Michelson's
BOOK
OF
WORLD BASEBALL
RECORDS

by

COURT MICHELSON

D1398947

ADAMS PRESS
CHICAGO, ILLINOIS

Sports Records Bureau
P.O. Box 25
Glen Ellyn, Illinois 60138

ISBN: 0-934175-00-4

Printed in the United States of America

First Edition

10 9 8 7 6 5 4 3 2 1

Cover Design: Joan Hubbell

CONTENTS

1. BATTING BRIEFS.................................... 1

Highest Average ... .400 Hitters ... Lowest Average ... Most
Hits ... Longest Hitting Streaks ... Longest Hitless Streak
... Most One-Base Hits ... Most Two-Base Hits ... Most
Three-Base Hits ... Most Home Runs ... Evolution Of Home
Run Record ... Home Run, First Pitch ... Grand Slam, First
Game ... Oldest Player To Hit Home Run ... Youngest Player
To Hit Home Run ... Longest Home Run ... Fungo Hitting ...
Most Runs Batted In ... Triple Crown ... Hitting For The
Cycle...Most Bases On Balls...Most Strikeouts ... Most Foul
Balls ... Designated Hitters ... Pinch-Hitters ...
Switch-Hitters ... Batting Titles, Won By Pitchers ...
Twenty-Game Winners Who Batted Over .300 ... Batting
Helmets

2. PITCHING PERFORMANCES................................ 23

Most Games ... Most Games Won ... Most Games Lost ... Most
Scoreless Innings ... Lowest ERA ... Highest ERA ... Most
Strikeouts ... Most Bases On Balls ... Fewest Pitches,
Game ... Most Wild Pitches ... Fastest Pitcher ... No-Hit
Games ... Perfect Games ... Relief Pitching ... Most
Saves ... Ultimate Relief Performance ... Longest Relief
Performance ... First Pitching Machine ... Ambidextrous
Players ... Blooper Pitch ... Change-Up ... Curve Ball ...
Emery Ball ... Fork Ball ... Knuckleball ... Screwball ...
Shine Ball ... Slider ... Spitball ... Submarine Pitch

3. FIELDING FEATS...................................... 45

All-Time Gold Glove Team ... Most Putouts ... Most As-
sists ... Fewest Chances Accepted, Game ... Most Double
Plays ... Unassisted Double Plays ... First Unassisted
Triple Play ... Unassisted Triple Plays ... Quadruple
Play ... Most Errors ... Fewest Errors ... Most Positions,
Game ... Defensive Shifts ... Five-Man Infield ...
Unglaub's Arc ... Record Altitude Catches ... Sinistral
Second Basemen ... Sinistral Catchers ... Longest Baseball
Throw ... First Gloves ... First Catcher's Mask ... First
Shin Guards

4.   RUNNING RECORDS.......................... 59

Most Runs Scored ... First Run ... Millionth Run ... Most
Stolen Bases ... Base Stealing Sweeps ... First Slide ...
Circling The Bases ... Wrong-Way Runners ... Attempted
Steal Of An Occupied Base ... Cutting Bases ... Fastest
Runner In Baseball History

5.   TEAM TOTALS.............................. 67

Major League Champions ... Most Pennants ... Baseball Dy-
nasties ... Most Wins ... Most Losses ... Highest
Percentage, Games Won ... Lowest Percentage, Games
Won ... Highest Batting Average ... Lowest Batting
Average ... Most Hits ... Most Home Runs ... Most Runs ...
Most Stolen Bases ... Most Double Plays ... Most Triple
Plays ... Longest Game ... Shortest Game ... Tripleheaders
... First Doubleheader ... First Team ... Early Air Travel
... First International Tour ... Women's Teams ... First
Women's League ... Early Black Teams ... The Old Negro
Leagues ... House of David Team ... All Nations Team ...
Family Teams...Alaskan Baseball ... Arctic Baseball ...
Australian Baseball ... Canadian Baseball ... Caribbean
Baseball ... Holland Baseball ... Italian Baseball ...
Japanese Baseball ... Mexican Baseball

6.   ARBITER ACHIEVEMENTS..................... 97

Hall Of Fame ... Most Seasons ... Most Leagues ... Most
Games ... Most Innings, One Day ... Most World Series ...
Most All-Star Games ... First Umpire ... Black
Umpires ... Canadian Umpires ... Electric Umpires ...
Largest Umpires ... Oldest Umpires ... Smallest Umpires ...
Women Umpires ... Youngest Umpires ... Hand Signals ...
First Umpire School ... First Umpire To Wear Glasses ...
Umpire Uniforms ... First Chest Protector ... Baseball
Rubbing Mud ... Whisk Broom ... Players Who Became
Umpires ... Umpire Expelled For Fixing Games ... Most
Ejections, Game

7.   MISCELLANEOUS MARKS..................... 109

Most Seasons ... Most Games ... Most Valuable Players ...
First All-Star Team ... College Baseball ... First Indoor
Game ... Night Baseball ... First Radio Broadcast ... First
Televised Game ... Spring Training ... First League ...
First Minor League ... Little League ... Six-Man
Baseball ... Welsh Baseball ... Largest Field ... Ballpark
Innovations ... Attendance Records ... Stadium Longevity

Records ... Seventh-Inning Stretch ... First Baseball Uni-
forms ... Uniform Numbers ... First Players To Wear Glasses
... Mustaches & Beards ... Colored Baseballs ... Bats ...
Baseball Cards...Candy Bars ... Stamps ... First Baseball
Movie ... Presidential Attendance ... Baseball Clowns ...
Black Players ... Canadian Players ... First Professional
Player ... Hawaiian Players ... Heaviest Players ... Indian
Players ... Italian Players ... Japanese Players ... Jewish
Players ... Latin-American Players ... Mexican Players ...
Oldest Players...Players Who Became Congressmen...Russian
Players ... Scandinavian Players ... Shortest Players ...
Tallest Players ... Women Players ... Youngest Players ...
Top Ten Managers ... First Black Managers ... First
Latin-American Manager ... Oldest Manager ... Youngest
Manager ... First Coach

8.   TRAGEDIES, HANDICAPS & COMEBACKS..................... 146

First Baseball Fatality ... The Ray Chapman Incident ...
Other Fatalities ... Near Fatalities ... Player Deaths
During Season ... War Casualties ... Comebacks And
Attempted Comebacks ... One-Armed Players ... One-Legged
Players ... Deaf Players ... One-Eyed Players ... Other
Handicapped Players

INDEX.. 161

INTRODUCTION

Michelson's Book of World Baseball Records is the first attempt ever made to combine the greatest recorded performances and contributions of the major leagues, the minor leagues, the old Negro leagues, as well as the Japanese, Mexican, Holland and Italian leagues into one publication. Many of the records in this book are being presented to today's fans for the first time. For the average baseball enthusiast, little is known of the baseball world outside of the majors. It is hoped that this book will help to somewhat fill that void.

Much of the enjoyment of being a baseball fan is having the opportunity to examine and compare the records. This not only provides a sense of history and appreciation for the game, but also stimulates interesting discussion and initiates questions and debates that will, no doubt, live forever.

By its very nature, baseball has always been a statistically oriented game. John Culkin, in a New York Times article describing the importance of records and statistics, stated that, "I don't think baseball could survive without all the statistical appurtenances involved in calculating pitching, hitting and fielding percentages. Some people could do without the games as long as they got the box scores."

This book does not attempt to detract from the magnitude of major league records, but merely presents the outstanding achievements in professional baseball history, regardless of the league in which they were established. Of course, players that have set major league marks, did so against the world's greatest teams and players. But in many instances, these are not "world records", as many have been surpassed in other leagues.

Major league records are referred to in this book as those that were performed in the following:

National League (1876-1984), American League (1901-1984), American Association (1882-1891), Union Association (1884), Players' League (1890) and Federal League (1914-1915).

It should also be noted that discrepancies in the various major league record books are due primarily to the fact that statistics before 1900 were not always recorded with the accuracy that they are today. Many have also been revised by researchers according to present-day rules and standards. The early totals, therefore, are not always agreed upon. Another reason is that not all six leagues are universally accepted as having been "major".

Record setting performances are often directly affected by a number of different variables. Among the most significant of these is probably the caliber of competition within a league. Since the levels of competition in the minor leagues vary greatly, an understanding of the classification system is important when evaluating and comparing records.

In 1901, the National Association of Professional Baseball Leagues was founded as the governing body of minor league baseball. It was at this time, that the classification system was established to assure more equal competition. The minors were then divided into four classes: A,B,C and D. In 1908, the American Association, the Eastern (International) League and the Pacific Coast League were given an AA rating, and later AAA in 1946. This system was completely revised in 1963 and today, the leagues are classified as either AAA, AA, A or R (rookie) leagues.

If the foreign leagues were to be classified, the Japanese Central and Pacific Leagues would probably be given an AAA-1 rating; halfway between Triple-A and the majors. According to several sources, the Mexican League, though officially rated as Triple-A, is actually closer to Double-A level of competition. The Holland and Italian Leagues might both rate an A classification.

Except for minor rule changes and equipment innovations, the game of baseball has remained relatively unchanged for the last fifty to sixty years. For this reason, many of baseball's records have been able to retain their significance over the years.

Record performances of seasons past seem to be brought back to life whenever a present-day player approaches one. When Pete Rose hit in 44 consecutive games in 1978, he equaled the National League record of Willie Keeler, set 81 years before, and connected the present with the past.

The "world" records found in this book may have been established against various levels of competition, but they are, nevertheless, the greatest statistics to have yet been researched and verified. It is also quite possible that some of them will never be surpassed, as many have already withstood the test of time.

In addition to records in most of the major categories of batting, pitching, fielding, baserunning and team performances, three additional chapters have also been added to recognize often neglected areas of baseball history. The Miscellaneous Marks chapter is a compilation of baseball trivia, covering everything from spring training to Little League. Included are little-known facts and "firsts" that are also an important part of the game's heritage. Michelson's Book of World Baseball Records also recognizes the contributions made by umpires, and is the first book to include extensive umpire records.

A final (non-record) chapter has been included to pay tribute to those forgotten players that met with tragedy, and to those who overcame near-insurmountable obstacles to reach greater heights. It should be remembered that the heroes are not only the players that set records, but also those who, by their courage and determination, provide inspiration for others.

It is hoped that this book will enlighten fans to different aspects of baseball and make the game that much more enjoyable to them. Michelson's Book of World Baseball Records is dedicated to each and every fan, for without them, there would be no professional baseball.

Court Michelson

ACKNOWLEDGEMENTS

We would like to thank the hundreds of baseball fans, researchers, administrators, sportswriters and ex-ballplayers who contributed to this project, particularly the many knowledgeable members of the Society for American Baseball Research (SABR), with whom we have exchanged and shared information over the years.

It has been through the efforts of SABR researchers that many of the minor league career totals have been recently compiled and are now accessible to today's fans. This organization, as well as Robert W. Peterson, for his history of Negro league baseball in Only The Ball Was White, are to be commended for reviving memories of players whose career accomplishments had long been forgotten.

The source for the majority of the major league career and season records was The Baseball Encyclopedia (Macmillan Publishing Co.), which has become the standard reference book for baseball researchers.

A special thanks is extended to SABR member Jerry Jackson for supplying many of the colorful minor league team nicknames.

Note: It is understood that no baseball publication can claim to include every record and notable performance of the last 140 years. We, therefore, welcome correspondence concerning any verifiable additions or corrections which deserve to be included in the next edition.

Sports Records Bureau
Dept. BB
P.O. Box 25
Glen Ellyn, IL   60138

Chapter One

BATTING BRIEFS

HIGHEST BATTING AVERAGE, LIFETIME

The highest batting average ever compiled in a major league career is .367 by Ty Cobb in twenty-four seasons with the Detroit Tigers and Philadelphia Athletics (1905-1928). Generally regarded as one of the greatest hitters in baseball history, he also led the American League twelve times in batting.

The all-time minor league record is .370 by outfielder Ike Boone, who played for ten different teams between 1920-1936. During his brief major league career he batted .319. (Source: Minor League Baseball Stars, Society for American Baseball Research).

In the old Negro leagues, career averages such as .408 by John Beckwith (1919-1934); .395 by Jud Wilson (1924-1945); and .391 by Josh Gibson (1930-1946) were compiled.

HIGHEST BATTING AVERAGE, SEASON

Since 1900, the highest batting average ever compiled in one full minor league season is .477. This was accomplished by Walter Malmquist of the York Prohibitionists (Class D Nebraska State League) during the 1913 season. The only time that this record has been approached was in 1978, when Gary Redus of the Billings Mustangs came within four hits of surpassing it. He batted .462 in the Class A Pioneer League that year.

Hugh Duffy, a five-foot-seven-inch center-fielder, hit for the highest average in a single major league season, .438, while playing for Boston (N.L.) in 1894.

1

BATTING BRIEFS

MAJOR LEAGUE .400 HITTERS (since 1900)

.424 Rogers Hornsby, St. Louis (N.L.), 1924
.422 Nap Lajoie, Philadelphia (A.L.), 1901
.420 Ty Cobb, Detroit (A.L.), 1911
.420 George Sisler, St. Louis (A.L.), 1922
.410 Ty Cobb, Detroit (A.L.), 1912
.408 Joe Jackson, Cleveland (A.L.), 1911
.407 George Sisler, St. Louis (A.L.), 1920
.406 Ted Williams, Boston (A.L.), 1941
.403 Harry Heilmann, Detroit (A.L.), 1923
.403 Rogers Hornsby, St. Louis (N.L.), 1925
.401 Ty Cobb, Detroit (A.L.), 1922
.401 Rogers Hornsby, St. Louis (N.L.), 1922
.401 Bill Terry, New York (N.L.), 1930

LOWEST BATTING AVERAGE, SEASON (excluding pitchers)
                  (minimum - 100 AB)

.095 Sandy Nava, Providence (N.L.), 1884
.096 Mike Jordan, Pittsburgh (N.L.), 1890
.108 Ben Egan, Cleveland (A.L.), 1915
.112 John Humphries, New York (N.L.), 1883
.117 Gracie Pearce, Columbus (A.A.), New York (N.L.), 1883
.121 Dwain Anderson, St. Louis, San Diego (N.L.), 1973
.122 George Baker, St. Louis (N.L.), 1885
.122 Frank O'Rourke, Boston (N.L.), 1912
.123 Norm Schlueter, Cleveland (A.L.), 1944
.124 Bill Killefer, St. Louis (A.L.), 1910

MOST HITS, LIFETIME

     Ty Cobb, who played for the Detroit Tigers and Philadelphia
Athletics from 1905-1928, had 4,191 hits during his career, the
most ever collected by a major league player.

2

BATTING BRIEFS

The minor league record is 3,617 by Spencer Harris, an outfielder who played for ten different teams between 1921-1948. (Source: Minor League Baseball Stars, SABR)

In the major leagues, there have been just 15 players who have collected 3,000 or more base hits:

4,191	Ty Cobb (1905-1928)
4,097	Pete Rose (1963-1984)
3,771	Hank Aaron (1954-1976)
3,630	Stan Musial (1941-1963)
3,515	Tris Speaker (1907-1928)
3,430	Honus Wagner (1897-1917)
3,419	Carl Yastrzemski (1961-1983)
3,311	Eddie Collins (1906-1930)
3,283	Willie Mays (1951-1973)
3,251	Nap Lajoie (1896-1916)
3,152	Paul Waner (1926-1945)
3,081	Cap Anson (1876-1897)
3,023	Lou Brock (1961-1979)
3,007	Al Kaline (1953-1974)
3,000	Roberto Clemente (1955-1972)

MOST HITS, SEASON

The all-time record of 325 hits was set in 1923 by Paul Strand, an outfielder for the Salt Lake City Bees of the Pacific Coast League (194 games). Strand had previously played in the majors as a pitcher for the Boston Braves.

In 1920, first baseman George Sisler of the St. Louis Browns set the major league record for the most hits in one season, 257 (154 games). He also led the league that year with a .407 average.

BATTING BRIEFS

LONGEST HITTING STREAKS

The longest hitting streak ever recorded is one of 69 consecutive games by Joe Wilhoit, an outfielder for the Wichita Wolves (Class A Western League), in 1919. He led the league with a .422 average and finished the season with the Boston Red Sox.

In 1941, Joe DiMaggio of the world champion New York Yankees set a major league mark when he hit in 56 consecutive games. Eight years earlier, he had hit in 61 straight while playing for the San Francisco Seals in the Pacific Coast League.

(Major league players - CAPITALIZED)

69	Joe Wilhoit, Wichita, 1919	
61	Joe DiMaggio, San Francisco, 1933	
56	JOE DIMAGGIO, NEW YORK, 1941	
55	Roman Mejias, Waco, 1954	
50	Otto Pahlman, Danville, 1922	
49	Jack Ness, Oakland, 1915	
49	Harry Chozen, Mobile, 1945	
46	Johnny Bates, Nashville, 1925	
44	WILLIE KEELER, BALTIMORE, 1897	
44	Jim Oglesby, Los Angeles, 1933	
44	PETE ROSE, CINCINNATI, 1978	

LONGEST HITLESS STREAK

Bob Buhl, a pitcher for the Milwaukee Braves and Chicago Cubs, established a major league futility record when he failed to get a hit in 42 consecutive games. During that streak, from 1961-1963, he went to bat 88 times without getting a hit.

MOST HITS, CONSECUTIVE

In the Negro American League, outfielder Rap Dixon of the

4

BATTING BRIEFS

Baltimore Black Sox collected 14 consecutive hits during a series against the Homestead Grays in 1929.

Also in 1929, George Quellich of the Reading Keystones had a streak of 15 straight hits against Toronto and Montreal in the International League.

Third baseman Pinky Higgins of the Boston Red Sox set the major league record when he collected 12 straight hits against Chicago and Detroit pitchers in 1938. Walt Dropo, first baseman for the Detroit Tigers, duplicated this effort in 1952 by hitting New York and Washington 12 consecutive times.

MOST HITS, GAME

The major league record for the most hits in a 9-inning game is 7, by catcher Wilbert Robinson of the Baltimore Orioles on June 10, 1892 against St. Louis.

This record was equaled 83 years later by Panamanian-born second baseman Rennie Stennett of the Pittsburgh Pirates. On September 16, 1975, he went 7-for-7 in a 22-0 victory over Chicago.

In an 18-inning game, shortstop Johnny Burnett of the Cleveland Indians collected 9 hits in 11 at-bats. He had seven singles and two doubles in his team's 18-17 loss to Philadelphia on July 10, 1932.

MOST HITS, INNING

The major league record for the most hits in one inning is 3, held by the following players:

Tom Burns, Chicago (N.L.), Sept. 6, 1883
Fred Pfeffer, Chicago (N.L.), Sept. 6, 1883
Ned Williamson, Chicago (N.L.), Sept. 6, 1883
Gene Stephens, Boston (A.L.), June 18, 1953

BATTING BRIEFS

The hits by Burns, Pfeffer and Williamson took place in the record 18-run seventh inning against Detroit. Stephens collected his hits in the seventh inning against Detroit, in which the Red Sox scored 17 runs.

MOST ONE-BASE HITS, LIFETIME

3,082 is the major league record for the most one-base hits in a career. It was achieved by Pete Rose, while playing for Cincinnati, Philadelphia and Montreal between 1963-1984. He also holds the National League record for the most singles in a season by a switch-hitter (181 in 1973).

The minor league mark is 2,944 by Eddie Hock, who played for twelve different clubs between 1920-1942. (Source: Minor League Baseball Stars, SABR)

MOST TWO-BASE HITS, LIFETIME

The career record for the most two-base hits in the major leagues is 793 by Tris Speaker, who played center field for four different teams between 1907-1928. Speaker established another record by leading the majors in doubles for seven seasons. During his career, nearly one-quarter of his hits went for two bases.

The minor league record of 743 was compiled by outfielder Spencer Harris, while playing for ten different clubs between 1921-1948. (Source: Minor League Baseball Stars, SABR)

MOST TWO-BASE HITS, SEASON

The all-time record of 100 doubles in one season was set in 1924 by five-foot-seven-inch outfielder Lyman Lamb of the Tulsa

BATTING BRIEFS

Oilers in the Class A Western League (168 games). No player in any league has ever come within 25 of this record.

Earl Webb, a right-fielder for the Boston Red Sox, established the major league record of 67 doubles in 1931 (151 games).

MOST TWO-BASE HITS, GAME

The professional record was first set on May 27, 1921, when Jim Blakesley of the Wichita Wolves hit 5 doubles in a Class A Western League game against Omaha. Les Bell of the Houston Buffaloes hit 5 consecutive doubles in a Class A Texas League game against Dallas on May 28, 1923. The record was also equaled on July 2, 1933, when third baseman Bucky Walters of the Mission Reds hit 5 doubles in a Pacific Coast League game against San Francisco.

The major league record for the most two-base hits in one game is 4, held by thirty-four different players. The first was center-fielder John O'Rourke of Boston (N.L.) on September 15, 1880. The last player to hit 4 doubles was Rick Miller, a center-fielder for the Boston Red Sox, on May 11, 1981 in a game against Toronto.

MOST THREE-BASE HITS, LIFETIME

Sam Crawford, an outfielder who played for the Cincinnati Reds and Detroit Tigers, hit a major league record 312 triples during his career (1899-1917). He also holds the record for leading the major leagues 5 times. Crawford is the only major leaguer to have hit 300 or more triples. In the minors, only two players ever reached the 200 mark.

BATTING BRIEFS

MOST THREE-BASE HITS, SEASON

The greatest number of triples hit in one season is 36, by center-fielder Owen Wilson of the Pittsburgh Pirates in 1912. During that season, he set another mark by hitting 6 triples in five consecutive games.

Jack Cross of the London Indians (Class B Michigan-Ontario League) connected for 32 triples in 1925, a minor league record.

In professional baseball there has been only one player (Pete Rose in 1961) in the last fifty-six years who has hit 30 triples in a season.

MOST THREE-BASE HITS, GAME

Shortstop George Strief of the Philadelphia Athletics established the record for the most triples in one game when he hit 4 on June 25, 1885. He also had a double in his team's 21-14 loss to Brooklyn. This was later duplicated on May 18, 1897 by third baseman Bill Joyce of the New York Giants in a game against Pittsburgh.

MOST HOME RUNS, LIFETIME

Josh Gibson is credited with hitting over 900 home runs in the old Negro leagues and the Caribbean winter leagues. He played catcher for the Pittsburgh Crawfords and Homestead Grays of the Negro National League (1930-1946) and in 1936, hit a record 84 home runs. This total also includes the home runs hit in exhibition games, many of which were against semi-pro clubs.

First baseman Sadaharu Oh of the Yomiuri (Tokyo) Giants hit a total of 868 home runs in the Japanese Central League from 1959-1980. In his twenty-two seasons, he led the league fifteen times and had a season high of 55 home runs in 1964.

BATTING BRIEFS

The major league record of 755 is held by Hank Aaron, who played outfield for the Milwaukee/Atlanta Braves and Milwaukee Brewers from 1954-1976. His actual total, though, including minor league (31), Puerto Rican Winter League (9), World Series (3), league playoffs (3) and All-Star games (2), also exceeds 800.

The only other player to have approached 800 is first baseman Hector Espino, who has played for the Monterrey Sultans of the Mexican League and the Hermosillo Orange Growers of the Mexican Pacific (Winter) League. He hit 791 home runs between 1960-1984. His best season was 1964 when he hit a combined total of 71 home runs. His totals are the result of having played year-round; over 175 games per year.

MOST HOME RUNS, SEASON

The minor league record of 72 was set in 1954 by first baseman Joe Bauman of the Roswell Rockets in the Class C Longhorn League (138 games). He also won the league's triple crown that year, hitting .400 and driving in 224 runs.

In 1961, right-fielder Roger Maris of the New York Yankees hit 61 home runs to break the major league record, which had been held by Babe Ruth for 34 years (161 games).

(Major league players - CAPITALIZED)

72	Joe Bauman, Roswell, 1954
69	Joe Hauser, Minneapolis, 1933
69	Bob Crues, Amarillo, 1948
66	Dick Stuart, Lincoln, 1956
64	Bob Lennon, Nashville, 1954
63	Joe Hauser, Baltimore, 1930
62	Moose Clabaugh, Tyler, 1926
62	Ken Guettler, Shreveport, 1956
61	ROGER MARIS, NEW YORK, 1961

BATTING BRIEFS

60   Tony Lazzeri, Salt Lake City, 1925
60   BABE RUTH, NEW YORK, 1927
60   Frosty Kennedy, Plainview, 1956

In the old Negro leagues, Josh Gibson's best seasons were 84 in 1936; 75 in 1931; and 72 in 1933 with the Pittsburgh Crawfords. It has also been reported that John Beckwith hit 72 in 1927, while Mule Suttles of the St. Louis Stars clouted 69 in 1929.

EVOLUTION OF MAJOR LEAGUE HOME RUN RECORD

5   George Hall, Philadelphia (N.L.), 1876
9   Charley Jones, Boston (N.L.), 1879
14   Harry Stovey, Philadelphia (A.A.), 1883
27   Ned Williamson, Chicago (N.L.), 1884
29   Babe Ruth, Boston (A.L.), 1919
54   Babe Ruth, New York (A.L.), 1920
59   Babe Ruth, New York (A.L.), 1921
60   Babe Ruth, New York (A.L.), 1927
61   Roger Maris, New York (A.L.), 1961

Perry Werden, first baseman for the Minneapolis Millers of the Western League, hit 45 home runs in 1895, a minor league record that stood for twenty-eight years.

MOST HOME RUNS, GAME

Nig Clarke, a Canadian-born catcher for Corsicana in the Class D Texas League, holds the all-time record of 8 home runs in a game. This unprecedented feat was performed against Texarkana on June 15, 1902.

The major league record for the most home runs in a 9-inning game is 4, held by seven different players. This was first achieved by Bobby Lowe, second baseman for Boston (N.L.), on May

30, 1894 in a game against Cincinnati. It was last performed by Willie Mays of the San Francisco Giants on April 30, 1961 against Milwaukee.

The first minor league player to hit 4 home runs in one game was John Crooks of the Omaha Omahogs on June 3, 1889 in a Western Association game against St. Paul.

MOST GAMES, CONSECUTIVE, HOME RUNS

In 1956, first baseman Dale Long of the Pittsburgh Pirates established a record by hitting a home run in 8 consecutive games. The previous professional record of 7 had been set in 1912 by Norman Munn of Richmond in the Class D Blue Grass League.

MOST HOME RUNS, INNING

On August 6, 1930, five-foot-six-inch outfielder Gene Rye of the Waco Cubs hit 3 home runs in the eighth inning of a game against Beaumont in the Class A Texas League. His team scored eighteen runs that inning and won the game, 22-4.

The major league record for the most home runs in an inning is 2, held by twenty-two different players. The first was Charley Jones, a left-fielder for Boston (N.L.), on June 10, 1880 in the eighth inning of a 19-3 win over Buffalo. It was last accomplished by Ray Knight of the Cincinnati Reds on May 13, 1980. He homered twice in the fifth inning against New York.

HOME RUN, FIRST MAJOR LEAGUE PITCH

On April 27, 1929, Clise Dudley, a relief pitcher for the Brooklyn Dodgers, became the first batter in major league history to hit a home run on the very first pitch thrown to him. It came in the third inning of a game against Philadelphia.

There have been ten other players who have also accomplished this feat:

Eddie Morgan, St. Louis (N.L.), 1936
Bill Lefebvre, Boston (A.L.), 1938
Clyde Vollmer, Cincinnati (N.L.), 1942
George Vico, Detroit (A.L.), 1948
Chuck Tanner, Milwaukee (N.L.), 1955
Bert Campaneris, Kansas City (A.L.), 1964
Brant Alyea, Washington (A.L.), 1965
Don Rose, California (A.L.), 1972
Gary Gaetti, Minnesota (A.L.), 1981
Andre David, Minnesota (A.L.), 1984

GRAND SLAM, FIRST MAJOR LEAGUE GAME

On April 21, 1898, in the second inning of a game against New York, pitcher Bill Duggleby of the Philadelphia Phillies became the only player in major league history to hit a bases-loaded home run in his first at-bat. He then went six years before hitting another homer.

Bobby Bonds, right-fielder for the San Francisco Giants, also hit a grand slam in his first major league game on June 25, 1968 against Los Angeles. Bond's hit came on his third at-bat.

HOME RUNS, CONSECUTIVE, FIRST MAJOR LEAGUE GAME

Left-fielder Bob Nieman of the St. Louis Browns set a major league record by hitting home runs in his first two at-bats in a game against Boston on September 14, 1951. The first home run came in the second inning, while the next shot was a 2-run homer in the third.

12

BATTING BRIEFS

OLDEST PLAYER TO HIT HOME RUN

The oldest player to hit a home run in major league competition is Jack Quinn, a relief pitcher for the Philadelphia Athletics, who homered in a game against St. Louis on June 27, 1930 at the age of 45 years, 357 days.

In an old-timers game on July 19, 1982, shortstop Luke Appling, playing for the American League team, hit a home run in the first inning. He was 75 years old.

YOUNGEST PLAYER TO HIT HOME RUN

Shortstop Tommy Brown of the Brooklyn Dodgers is the youngest player to have hit a home run in a major league game. He homered in the seventh inning of a game against Pittsburgh on August 20, 1945 at the age of 17 years, 257 days.

LONGEST HOME RUN

The all-time record for a measured home run is 618 feet by outfielder Roy Carlyle of the Oakland Oaks in a Pacific Coast League game on July 4, 1929. The closest that anyone has come to this mark was a 610-foot shot by Dick Stuart of the Lincoln Chiefs in a Class A Western League game in 1957.

The longest "measured" home run in a major league game is 573 feet. This was achieved by left-fielder Dave Nicholson of the Chicago White Sox on May 6, 1964 in a game against Kansas City.

On June 8, 1926, Babe Ruth of the New York Yankees hit a towering home run against Detroit that was claimed to have traveled 620 feet. Six-foot-six-inch outfielder Dave Kingman of the New York Mets hit a home run that was estimated to be 630 feet in a game against Chicago on April 14, 1976. Unfortunately, neither of these ever actually measured.

BATTING BRIEFS

FUNGO HITTING

The major league distance record of 447 feet was set at Yankee Stadium by Babe Ruth of the New York Yankees on July 31, 1929. This broke the old mark of 419'6" by Ed Walsh in 1911. Henry Miller of the Winnipeg Maroons (Class C Northern League) established the minor league record in 1916 when he hit a ball 438'2".

The world record is 503'3" by Walter Driver, Victorian Baseball Association of Melbourne, Australia, in 1945.

The greatest reported height attained on a fungo hit was established on April 12, 1965. During the pre-game workout, Ed Roebuck of the Philadelphia Phillies hit the ceiling of the Houston Astrodome above first base; a height of 190 feet.

(The term "fungo" comes from the Scottish word, fung; to snap or toss into the air.)

MOST RUNS BATTED IN, LIFETIME

The greatest number of runs batted in by a major league player is 2,297 by Hank Aaron, who played for the Milwaukee/Atlanta Braves and the Milwaukee Brewers between 1954-1976. He led the major leagues in this category four times during his career.

In the Japanese Central League, Sadaharu Oh of the Yomiuri (Tokyo) Giants drove in 2,170 runs between 1959-1980. During his career, he had fourteen 100-RBI seasons.

MOST RUNS BATTED IN, SEASON

Bob Crues, an outfielder for the Amarillo Gold Sox of the Class C West Texas-New Mexico League, set an all-time record in 1948 by driving in 254 runs (140 games). He also batted .404

and hit 69 home runs in what is considered by many to have been the greatest single season by any player.

In 1930, center-fielder Hack Wilson of the Chicago Cubs drove in 190 runs, a major league record (155 games). He also hit a National League record 56 home runs that season.

MOST GAMES, CONSECUTIVE, RUNS BATTED IN

In 1922, first baseman Ray Grimes of the Chicago Cubs set a major league record when he collected an RBI in 17 consecutive games. During this streak, he drove in a total of twenty-seven runs.

MOST RUNS BATTED IN, GAME

The record for the most RBIs in one game is 16, by catcher Nig Clarke of the Corsicana Oil City. This took place on June 15, 1902 in a Class D Texas League game against Texarkana in which he homered eight times.

The major league standard is 12, recorded by Jim Bottomley, first baseman for the St. Louis Cardinals, in a game against Brooklyn on September 16, 1924. He went 6-for-6 that day, including two home runs.

MOST RUNS BATTED IN, INNING

On August 6, 1930, outfielder Gene Rye of the Waco Cubs established an all-time record by driving in 8 runs during the eighth inning of a Texas League game against Beaumont. He led off the inning with a solo home run, and then followed with a 3-run homer and a grand slam.

This record was equaled on May 2, 1947, when first baseman Ken Myers of the Las Vegas Wranglers hit two grand slams in one inning of a Class C Sunset League game against Ontario. On June 30, 1983, left-fielder Lance Junker of the Redwood Pioneers also duplicated this effort. He hit two grand slams in the ninth inning of a Class A California League game against Reno.

The major league record of 7 was set by first baseman Ed Cartwright of the St. Louis Browns in the third inning of a game against Philadelphia on September 23, 1890.

TRIPLE CROWN WINNERS (Major league)

		HR	RBI	AVG.
1922	Rogers Hornsby, St. Louis (N.L.)	42	152	.401
1925	Rogers Hornsby, St. Louis (N.L.)	39	143	.403
1933	Jimmie Foxx, Philadelphia (A.L.)	48	163	.356
1933	Chuck Klein, Philadelphia (N.L.)	28	120	.368
1934	Lou Gehrig, New York (A.L.)	49	165	.363
1937	Joe Medwick, St. Louis (N.L.)	31	154	.374
1942	Ted Williams, Boston (A.L.)	36	137	.356
1947	Ted Williams, Boston (A.L.)	32	114	.343
1956	Mickey Mantle, New York (A.L.)	52	130	.353
1966	Frank Robinson, Baltimore (A.L.)	49	122	.316
1967	Carl Yastrzemski, Boston (A.L.)	44	121	.326

Recent research has found that unofficial Triple Crowns were won by Paul Hines, Providence (1878); Hugh Duffy, Boston (1894); Nap Lajoie, Philadelphia (1901); Ty Cobb, Detroit (1909); and Heinie Zimmerman, Chicago (1912). Prior to 1920, runs batted in were not recorded as official statistics.

HITTING FOR THE CYCLE

The cycle; a single, double, triple and home run in one game has been accomplished over 200 times in major league competition. The first player to hit for the cycle was left-fielder George Hall of the Philadelphia Athletics on June 14, 1876. It was last performed by Dwight Evans of the Boston Red Sox in a 9-6 victory over Seattle on June 28, 1984.

Long John Reilly of the Cincinnati Reds, Bob Meusel of the New York Yankees and Babe Herman of the Brooklyn Dodgers each hit for the cycle three times during their careers.

MOST BASES ON BALLS, SEASON

Pete Hughes, an outfielder for the Las Vegas Wranglers of the Class C Sunset League, collected 210 walks in 1949 (123 games) to break the all-time record which he had set the previous year. During his career, Hughes collected more walks than hits.

Right-fielder Babe Ruth of the New York Yankees walked 170 times (including 80 intentional passes) in 1923 to set a major league record (152 games). He also had 8 more in the World Series that year.

Sadaharu Oh of the Yomiuri (Tokyo) Giants walked 166 times during the 1974 season (130 games). Oh also holds the all-time career record of 2,504 bases on balls (1959-1980).

MOST GAMES, CONSECUTIVE, BASES ON BALLS

First baseman Roy Cullenbine of the Detroit Tigers played in 22 consecutive games in 1947 in which he received at least one base on balls.

MOST STRIKEOUTS, SEASON

The all-time strikeout record is 220 by Wes Kent, a first baseman for the San Jose Bees of the Class A California League in 1984 (137 games).

BATTING BRIEFS

Right-fielder Bobby Bonds of the San Francisco Giants established a major league record when he struck out 189 times in 1970 (157 games). This broke his own record of 187 set in 1969.

MOST GAMES, CONSECUTIVE, NO STRIKEOUTS

In 1929, Cleveland third baseman Joe Sewell set a major league record by playing in 115 games without striking out. During his fourteen-year career, he struck out only 114 times while compiling a .312 average.

Some sources claim that outfielder Willie Keeler of the Baltimore Orioles played 128 games in 1898 without striking out.

MOST FOUL BALLS, CONSECUTIVE (since 1900)

In a Class A Southern Association game on July 9, 1934, outfielder Eddie Rose of the champion New Orleans Pelicans fouled off 19 consecutive pitches thrown by Hank Hulvey before grounding out.

Chicago shortstop Luke Appling, in a game against Detroit, fouled off 14 consecutive pitches. On the fifteenth pitch, frustrated pitcher Dizzy Trout threw his glove instead of the ball.

Prior to 1894, batters were allowed to bunt foul with two strikes and any foul ball that was not bunted was not considered a strike.

DESIGNATED HITTERS

The designated hitter rule was originally proposed by National League president John Heydler in 1928. Forty-one years later, it was tested in the Eastern, International, New-York-

Penn and Texas Leagues during the 1969 season. The rule was finally adopted after four years by the American League as a 3-year experiment.

Larry Hisle of the Minnesota Twins became the first major leaguer to appear as a DH. He hit two homers and drove in seven runs in a Grapefruit League exhibition game against Pittsburgh on March 6, 1973.

Ron Blomberg of the New York Yankees holds the distinction of being the first DH in a regular season game. Against Boston on opening day (April 6, 1973) he drew a walk in the first inning with the bases loaded. He was 1-for-3 that day.

American League DH of the Year

1984	Dave Kingman, Oakland
1983	Greg Luzinski, Chicago
1982	Hal McRae, Kansas City
1981	Greg Luzinski, Chicago
1980	Hal McRae, Kansas City
1979	Willie Horton, Seattle
1978	Rusty Staub, Detroit
1977	Jim Rice, Boston
1976	Hal McRae, Kansas City
1975	Willie Horton, Detroit
1974	Tommy Davis, Baltimore
1973	Orlando Cepeda, Boston

PINCH-HITTERS

The first pinch-hitter in the major leagues was Mickey Welch of the New York Giants. He batted for pitcher Hank O'Day in the sixth inning of a game against Indianapolis on August 10, 1889, and struck out.

The most prolific pinch-hitter in major league history was Manny Mota. He played for four different teams between 1962-1980 and collected a record 150 pinch hits during his career. Mota also played twenty seasons in the Dominican Republic Winter League, where he compiled a record .333 average.

SWITCH-HITTERS

The first switch-hitter was Bob Ferguson, manager and third baseman for the New York Mutuals in 1871. He played in the old National Association from 1871-1875 and in the National League from 1876-1883.

Probably the greatest switch-hitting feat of all-time took place in the International League on May 3, 1961. In the eighth inning of a game against Jersey City, Ellis Burton of the Toronto Maple Leafs hit two home runs; one from each side of the plate. This accomplishment has since been duplicated by Gary Pellant of the Alexandria Dukes on April 30, 1979 in a Class C Carolina League game against Salem.

Switch-Hitting Batting Champions

.372 Tommy Tucker, Baltimore (A.A.), 1889
.353 Mickey Mantle, New York (A.L.), 1956
.335 Pete Rose, Cincinnati (N.L.), 1968
.348 Pete Rose, Cincinnati (N.L.), 1969
.338 Pete Rose, Cincinnati (N.L.), 1973
.332 Willie Wilson, Kansas City (A.L.) 1982

BATTING TITLES, WON BY PITCHERS

In 1886, Guy Hecker of the Louisville Colonels became the only pitcher in major league history to win a batting crown. He hit .342 to edge out teammate Pete Browning (.340) for the title. Hecker also won 27 games that year.

Several pitchers in the minor leagues have also won batting titles. The last to accomplish this was Roy Sanner of the Houma

20

Indians.   In 1948, he won the triple crown, batted .386 and won 21 games as a pitcher in the Class D Evangeline League.

Giulio Glorioso of the Rome Senators won the Italian League batting title in 1960 when he hit .423, and also won 13 games. He was traded to Milan the next year, and again won the batting crown.   He hit .444, while posting an 18-0 record as a pitcher.

In the Mexican League, Martin Dihigo batted .387 to lead the league.   He also won 18 games as he led the Veracruz Eagles to the pennant in 1938.

20-GAME WINNERS WHO BATTED OVER .300

There have been 47 pitchers in major league history who have won twenty games and also batted over .300 in the same year (minimum - 100 AB).   The top ten:

.381	Curt Davis, St. Louis (N.L.), 1939
.361	George Uhle, Cleveland (A.L.), 1923
.359	Don Newcombe, Brooklyn (N.L.), 1955
.350	Catfish Hunter, Oakland (A.L.), 1971
.347	Wes Ferrell, Boston (A.L.), 1935
.346	Wilbur Cooper, Pittsburgh (N.L.), 1924
.346	Johnny Sain, Boston (N.L.), 1947
.344	Jack Stivetts, Boston (N.L.), 1896
.343	Carl Mays, New York (A.L.), 1921
.342	Guy Hecker, Louisville (A.A.), 1886

BATTING HELMETS

In a game against Cincinnati on June 18, 1907, Roger Bresnahan of the New York Giants was struck in the head by a pitch.   During the 3-1/2 weeks that he was out of action, he developed a leather headguard that could be worn over his hat while batting.   Unfortunately, this idea was not well received and was soon abandoned.

BATTING BRIEFS

The next appearance of head protectors took place on May 29, 1937 when the Des Moines Demons and Cedar Rapids Raiders wore polo helmets in a Class A Western League game.

In 1941, the Brooklyn Dodgers wore specially designed hats that contained a two-sectioned plastic protector. The first player to wear one of these in a game was Pee Wee Reese on March 8, 1941 in a spring exhibition against Cleveland. The next season the Class B Inter-State League required each of its teams to purchase them. Their use, though, was not compulsory.

The first Negro league player to wear a helmet was shortstop Willie Wells of the Newark Eagles (Negro National League). Following a severe beaning in 1942, he wore a construction worker's hardhat while batting.

The modern fiberglass helmets were invented in 1950, and two years later, the Pittsburgh Pirates became the first team to use them. Their use did not become mandatory in the major leagues, though, until 1958.

Chapter Two

PITCHING PERFORMANCES

MOST GAMES, LIFETIME

The most games ever pitched in the major leagues is 1,070 by relief pitcher Hoyt Wilhelm. He played for nine different teams between 1952-1969, before retiring at the age of 49.

Bill Thomas, who pitched for twenty-two different teams from 1926-1952, appeared in 1,015 minor league games. Thomas was 47 when he retired. (Source: Minor League Baseball Stars, SABR)

MOST GAMES WON, LIFETIME

The winningest pitcher in major league history was Cy Young. He played for five different teams between 1890-1911, and won a total of 511 games during his career. Young had 14 consecutive seasons with 20 victories or more, including five with more than 30 wins. He also threw three no-hitters and a perfect game.

The Japanese League record is 400 by Masaichi Kaneda, who pitched for the Kokutetsu Swallows and the Yomiuri (Tokyo) Giants between 1950-1969. During his career, he won 20 or more games fourteen times, including two 30-win seasons.

The minor league record of 383 was set by Bill Thomas from 1926-1952. (Source: Minor League Baseball Stars, SABR)

There have been just 16 pitchers in major league history who have won 300 or more games:

> 511 Cy Young (1890-1911)
> 416 Walter Johnson (1907-1927)

PITCHING PERFORMANCES

373   Christy Mathewson (1900-1916)
373   Grover Alexander (1911-1930)
363   Warren Spahn (1942-1965)
361   Pud Galvin (1879-1892)
360   Kid Nichols (1890-1906)
344   Tim Keefe (1880-1893)
327   Eddie Plank (1901-1917)
326   John Clarkson (1882-1894)
314   Gaylord Perry (1962-1983)
313   Steve Carlton (1965-1984)
311   Mickey Welch (1880-1892)
308   Old Hoss Radbourn (1880-1891)
300   Lefty Grove (1925-1941)
300   Early Wynn (1939-1963)

MOST GAMES WON, SEASON

The major league record for the most games won in a season is 60 by Old Hoss Radbourn of the Providence Grays in 1884. He also added 3 more victories in the World Series. This was accomplished in an era (1881-1893) when the pitching distance to home plate was 50 feet.

Since 1893, the most wins by a major league pitcher is 41 by Jack Chesbro of New York (A.L.) in 1904. In the Japanese leagues, Victor Starfin won 42 games in 1939 to lead the Yomiuri (Tokyo) Giants to the pennant. In 1961, Kazuhisa Inao of the Nishitetsu Lions also won 42 games.

Major league - before 1893

60   Old Hoss Radbourn, Providence, 1884
53   John Clarkson, Chicago, 1885
52   Guy Hecker, Louisville, 1884
49   John Clarkson, Boston, 1889
48   Charlie Buffinton, Boston, 1884
48   Old Hoss Radbourn, Providence, 1883

24

PITCHING PERFORMANCES

47   John M. Ward, Providence, 1879

47   Matt Kilroy, Baltimore, 1887

46   Al Spalding, Chicago, 1876

46   Pud Galvin, Buffalo, 1884

46   Pud Galvin, Buffalo, 1883

Since 1893

(Major league players - CAPITALIZED)

42   Victor Starfin, Yomiuri Giants, 1939

42   Kazuhisa Inao, Nishitetsu Lions, 1961

41   JACK CHESBRO, NEW YORK, 1904

41   Stoney McGlynn, York/Steubenville, 1906

39   Doc Newton, Los Angeles, 1904

39   Rube Vickers, Seattle, 1906

39   ED WALSH, CHICAGO, 1908

38   George Boehler, Tulsa, 1922

38   Tadashi Sugiura, Nankai Hawks, 1959

37   Ham Iburg, San Francisco, 1901

37   Oscar Jones, Los Angeles, 1902

37   CHRISTY MATHEWSON, NEW YORK, 1908

In the old Negro leagues, Rube Foster of the Cuban Giants won 51 games in 1902. Jose Mendez of the Cuban Stars is credited with 44 wins in 1909. Cannonball Dick Redding of the Lincoln Giants won 43 in 1912 and, in 1939, Laymon Yokely of the Philadelphia Stars won 42.

MOST GAMES WON, CONSECUTIVE

Willie Foster of the Chicago American Giants won 26 consecutive games in Negro National League competition during the 1926 season. Baxter Sparks set a minor league record by winning 21 straight for Yazoo City of the Class D Delta League in 1904. He finished the season with a 25-8 record.

PITCHING PERFORMANCES

In 1888, Tim Keefe of the world champion New York Giants set a major league record by winning 19 consecutive games. Twenty-four years later, Rube Marquard, also of the New York Giants, won 19 in a row.

Extending over two seasons, Carl Hubbell of the New York Giants won 24 consecutive games while leading his team to pennants in 1936-1937. In the old National Association, Al Spalding won 24 straight for Boston in 1875.

MOST GAMES LOST, LIFETIME

The all-time minor league standard of 346 losses was set by Bill Thomas during his 25-year career from 1926-1952. (Source: Minor League Baseball Stars, SABR)

The major league record for the most games lost is 313 by Cy Young between 1890-1911. Surprisingly, he only had four losing seasons in his 22-year career.

MOST GAMES LOST, SEASON

John Coleman, pitching for the last-place Philadelphia Phillies in 1883, lost 48 games, a major league record. He did manage to win 12 that season. The next year he was traded and became an outfielder.

MOST GAMES LOST, CONSECUTIVE

George Haddock was the losing pitcher in 20 consecutive appearances for the Troy Trojans of the International Association in 1888, an all-time record.

The major league record was established by Jack Nabors of the 1916 Philadelphia Athletics (considered by many to have been one of the worst teams in major league history). He won his first start, but then lost the next 19.

During a period covering two seasons, Cliff Curtis of Boston (N.L.) lost 23 consecutive games (1910-1911). This record was also set with a last place team.

MOST SCORELESS INNINGS, CONSECUTIVE

In the Negro American League, Satchel Paige of the champion Kansas City Monarchs compiled a streak of 64 consecutive scoreless innings in 1946.

Don Drysdale of the Los Angeles Dodgers established the major league record in 1968 when he pitched 58 2/3 consecutive innings without allowing a run. This broke a fifty-five year old record held by Walter Johnson of the Washington Senators (56 in 1913). Johnson had also once pitched 75 consecutive scoreless innings in the semi-pro Snake River Valley League (Idaho) in 1907.

The minor league record of 55 had been established in 1907 by Irvin Wilhelm, while pitching for the Birmingham Barons of the Southern Association.

LOWEST EARNED RUN AVERAGE, SEASON

Bob Gibson of the St. Louis Cardinals recorded the lowest ERA in major league history for one season (300 innings minimum), 1.12 in 1968. He also was selected MVP that year; the last National League pitcher to be so honored.

HIGHEST EARNED RUN AVERAGE, SEASON

The highest ERA ever recorded by a major league pitcher is an astronomical 189.00. The first to accomplish this was John

Scheible of the Philadelphia Phillies in 1894. Fifty-one years later, this unenviable mark was equaled by Joe Cleary of the Washington Senators in 1945. Neither one of them ever pitched again in the majors.

MOST STRIKEOUTS, LIFETIME

The all-time record of 4,490 strikeouts was set in the Japanese leagues by Masaichi Kaneda. During his 20-year career (1950-1969), he averaged 225 strikeouts a season. For five consecutive seasons he struck out 300 or more batters.

The major league record for the most strikeouts is 3,874 by Nolan Ryan, who has pitched for New York, California and Houston from 1968-1984. He is also the only major leaguer to have ever recorded 300 or more strikeouts in three consecutive seasons.

George Brunet recorded 3,175 strikeouts in his minor league career, which began in 1953. He spent the last twelve seasons in the Mexican League, following his 15-year career in the majors (1956-1971).

The Italian League record of 2,884 strikeouts was established by Giulio Glorioso, who once had a tryout with the Cleveland Indians. He declined a contract offer in the U.S. and returned to Italy, where he pitched for four different teams between 1953-1974.

MOST STRIKEOUTS, SEASON

Major league - before 1893
(Pitching distance to home plate - 50 feet)

505 Matt Kilroy, Baltimore, 1886
499 Toad Ramsey, Louisville, 1886
483 One-Arm Daily, Washington, 1884
451 Dupee Shaw, Detroit/Boston, 1884

PITCHING PERFORMANCES

```
441   Old Hoss Radbourn, Providence, 1884
417   Charlie Buffinton, Boston, 1884
385   Guy Hecker, Louisville, 1884
374   Bill Sweeney, Baltimore, 1884
369   Pud Galvin, Buffalo, 1884
368   Mark Baldwin, Columbus, 1889
```

(Major league players - CAPITALIZED)

```
456   Bill Kennedy, Rocky Mount, 1946
418   Virgil Trucks, Andalusia, 1938
408   Rube Vickers, Seattle, 1906
401   Yutaka Enatsu, Hanshin Tigers, 1968
390   Doc Ayers, Richmond, 1913
389   Ed Albrecht, Pine Bluff, 1949
383   NOLAN RYAN, CALIFORNIA, 1973
382   SANDY KOUFAX, LOS ANGELES, 1965
376   Vean Gregg, Portland, 1910
367   NOLAN RYAN, CALIFORNIA, 1974
```

MOST STRIKEOUTS, GAME

The all-time record for the most strikeouts in a nine-inning game is held by Ron Necciai of the Bristol Twins (Class D Appalachian League). On May 13, 1952, he struck out the unbelievable total of 27 batters while pitching a no-hit game against Welch.

In 1955, Han Urbanus of Amsterdam established the Holland League record when he recorded 21 strikeouts in a nine-inning game. He also averaged fifteen strikeouts per game that season.

The greatest number of strikeouts thrown in a nine-inning major league game is 19, by the following:

Charlie Sweeney, Providence (N.L.), June 7, 1884
One-Arm Daily, Chicago (U.A.), July 7, 1884
Steve Carlton, St. Louis (N.L.), September 15, 1969

Tom Seaver, New York (N.L.), April 22, 1970
Nolan Ryan, California (A.L.), August 12, 1974

MOST STRIKEOUTS, EXTRA INNING GAME

On July 15, 1941, Hooks Iott of the Paragould Browns (Class D Northeast Arkansas League) set an all-time record by striking out 30 batters in a sixteen-inning game against Newport, the league champions that year.

The Italian League record of 29 strikeouts by Mike Romano of Renana was accomplished in a twelve-inning game against Rome in 1973.

Smokey Joe Williams of the Homestead Grays (Negro National League) struck out 27 in a twenty-inning victory over Kansas City on August 3, 1930.

Tom Cheney of the Washington Senators struck out 21 batters in a sixteen-inning game against Baltimore on September 12, 1962 to set a major league record.

MOST STRIKEOUTS, CONSECUTIVE

Mike Romano, pitching for Renana in the Italian League, set a record when he struck out 11 consecutive batters in a game against Torino in 1973. Several minor leaguers have also matched this total.

The major league record for the most strikeouts in a row is held by Tom Seaver of the New York Mets. He fanned the last 10 batters in a 2-1 victory over San Diego on April 22, 1970, breaking Mickey Welch's 86-year old record.

MOST STRIKEOUTS, INNING

Normally, three strikeouts would be enough to retire the

side, but in the case of a dropped third strike (passed ball) by the catcher, it sometimes requires more.

The record is held by Willie Mitchell of San Antonio, who struck out 7 batters in one inning of a Class C Texas League game against Houston in 1909. His catcher missed four third-strikes. Earlier that year, while pitching for Mississippi State, Mitchell had established a collegiate record by compiling 26 strikeouts in a nine-inning game.

The major league record for the most strikeouts in an inning is 4, held by seventeen different pitchers. The first to accomplish this feat was Bobby Mathews of the Philadelphia Athletics on September 30, 1885. It was last performed by Mario Soto of the Cincinnati Reds on May 17, 1984 in the third inning of a game against Chicago.

MOST BASES ON BALLS, LIFETIME

The record for the most walks allowed by a pitcher is 2,096 by Dick Barrett, who played for fourteen different minor league teams between 1925-1953. Despite this, he was still able to win 325 games during his career. (Source: Minor League Baseball Stars, SABR)

Nolan Ryan recorded the major league record of 2,091 walks in eighteen seasons with New York, California and Houston (1966,68-84). He also led the major leagues a record 7 times.

In the Japanese leagues, Masaichi Kaneda, who played for the Kokutetsu Swallows and Yomiuri (Tokyo) Giants between 1950-1969, walked a total of 1,809 batters.

MOST BASES ON BALLS, SEASON

Amos Rusie of the New York Giants set a major league record when he walked 289 batters in 1890 (67 games). Despite this lack of control, he was still able to win 29 games that season and also lead the majors in strikeouts.

The minor league record is 264 by Ed Frenick of the High Point Pointers (Class C Piedmont League) in 1923. The Italian League record of 199 walks was achieved by Giacomo Bertoni of Rimini in 1970 (25 games).

(Major league players - CAPITALIZED)

289 AMOS RUSIE, NEW YORK, 1890
274 MARK BALDWIN, COLUMBUS, 1889
267 AMOS RUSIE, NEW YORK, 1892
264 Ed Frenick, High Point, 1923
262 AMOS RUSIE, NEW YORK, 1891
262 Steve Dalkowski, Stockton, 1960
255 Jesse Burkett, Worcester, 1889
249 MARK BALDWIN, CHICAGO, 1890
237 Oscar Roettger, Sioux City, 1922
237 Bob Schulte, Riverside, 1948

MOST BASES ON BALLS, GAME

Bill DiBenedetto of the Hornell Dodgers (Class D P.O.N.Y. League) walked a record 21 batters in a 5-1 loss to Corning on July 3, 1951. This effort broke a thirty-six year old record which had been held by Harry Harper of the Minneapolis Millers.

The major league record for the most bases on balls in one game is 16, held by the following pitchers:

Bill George, New York (N.L.), May 30, 1887
George Van Haltren, Chicago (N.L.), June 27, 1887
Henry Gruber, Cleveland (P.L.), April 19, 1890
Bruno Haas, Philadelphia (A.L.), June 13, 1915

PITCHING PERFORMANCES

MOST BASES ON BALLS, INNING

Lefty Stanton of the Shreveport Sports set an all-time record when he walked 10 batters in one inning of a Class A Texas League game against Houston on May 14, 1925.

Dolly Gray of the Washington Senators established the major league record when he walked 8 batters in the second inning of a game against Chicago on August 28, 1909. Seven of those walks were consecutive, another record. Chicago scored six runs that inning and won, 6-4.

FEWEST PITCHES, GAME

The major league record for the fewest pitches thrown in a complete game was established by Red Barrett of the Boston Braves on August 10, 1944. He threw only 58 pitches while shutting out Cincinnati on two hits. He had no walks or strikeouts, and the game lasted only one hour and fifteen minutes. The previous record of 65 pitches was set by Slim Sallee of the Cincinnati Reds in 1919 against Brooklyn.

This total was matched by Bob Kipper of the Redwood Pioneers, while pitching a no-hitter against San Jose in the Class A California League on June 10, 1984.

MOST WILD PITCHES

On July 22, 1876, Johnny Ryan of the Louisville Colonels displayed an amazing lack of control as he threw 10 wild pitches against Chicago in his first, and only, major league game. The final score was 30-7.

Ray Gault of the Bakersfield Outlaws set a record on April 24, 1978 when he uncorked 8 wild pitches in the second inning of a Class A California League game against Reno.

PITCHING PERFORMANCES

In a Mexican League game on June 28, 1979, four consecutive wild pitches were thrown by Cy Acosta of the Aguascalientes Railworkers in the first inning against Cordoba.

FASTEST PITCHER

The radar gun, which clocks the velocity of a pitch, is a relatively new invention. It is, therefore, impossible to establish the fastest pitcher of all-time. Every era has had its "flame-thrower", from Amos Rusie in the 1890s to Nolan Ryan and J.R. Richard in the 1970s. Walter Johnson, Lefty Grove, Bob Feller, Smokey Joe Williams, Sandy Koufax and Steve Dalkowski have also been claimed, by different sources, to have been the hardest throwers.

The fastest official time for a pitched ball (excluding throws by mechanical pitching machines and trained elephants) is 100.9 m.p.h. by Nolan Ryan of the California Angels on August 20, 1974 at Anaheim Stadium. At this speed, after the ball leaves the pitcher's hand, it reaches the plate in .38 seconds.

In tests performed at West Point on May 23, 1930, Yankee pitcher Lou McEvoy's throw was timed at 102.27 m.p.h., and shortstop Mark Koenig's almost equaled that. The accuracy of this test, though, has been questioned. The average major league fastball is around 84-85 m.p.h.

In comparison, the fastest recorded pitch in softball is 108 m.p.h. by Jack Newman of Oxnard, California in 1962. The fastest pitch by a cricket bowler (pitcher) is 99.7 m.p.h. by Jeff Thompson of Australia in December, 1975.

NO-HIT GAMES

The first no-hitter in the major leagues was thrown by Joe Borden of Boston (N.L.) on May 23, 1876 when he defeated

Cincinnati, 8-0. (This game was not originally recorded as a no-hitter, as the official scorer had counted two bases on balls as hits.)

There have been over 200 no-hitters of at least nine innings pitched in major league competition. Nolan Ryan has thrown 5 in his career while pitching for the California Angels and Houston Astros; 1973 (two), 1974, 1975 and 1981.

In 1938, Johnny Vander Meer of the Cincinnati Reds became the only player in major league history to hurl 2 consecutive no-hitters.

NO-HIT GAME, FIRST START

There have been three pitchers in major league history who have accomplished the rare feat of throwing a no-hitter in their first starting assignment. The first was Ted Breitenstein of the St. Louis Browns, who defeated Louisville, 8-0, on October 4, 1891 without allowing a hit.

On October 15, 1892, Bumpus Jones of the Cincinnati Reds matched this effort by pitching a no-hitter against Pittsburgh in his first game. Bobo Holloman of the St. Louis Browns, on May 6, 1953, defeated Philadelphia, 6-0, on no hits.

PERFECT GAMES

In major league history, there have been twelve games pitched (of at least nine innings) in which no batter has reached first base:

        Lee Richmond, Worcester (N.L.), June 12, 1880
        John M. Ward, Providence (N.L.), June 17, 1880
        Cy Young, Boston (A.L.), May 5, 1904
        Addie Joss, Cleveland (A.L.), October 2, 1908
        Ernie Shore, Boston (A.L.), June 23, 1917

PITCHING PERFORMANCES

Charlie Robertson, Chicago (A.L.), April 30, 1922

Don Larsen, New York (A.L.), October 8, 1956

Jim Bunning, Philadelphia (N.L.), June 21, 1964

Sandy Koufax, Los Angeles (N.L.), September 9, 1965

Catfish Hunter, Oakland (A.L.), May 8, 1968

Len Barker, Cleveland (A.L.), May 15, 1981

Mike Witt, California (A.L.), September 30, 1984

Perfect games of less than nine innings have been pitched by Rube Vickers, Philadelphia (1907); Ed Karger, St. Louis (1907); Dean Chance, Minnesota (1967); and Dave Palmer, Montreal (1984).

The first recorded perfect game was pitched on August 17, 1876 by Pud Galvin of the St. Louis Reds. He defeated the Cass club of Detroit in an exhibition game, 1-0.

Dan McClellan of the Cuban X Giants became the first Negro league pitcher to hurl a perfect game on July 17, 1903. The first perfect game in the Mexican League was pitched by Ramiro Cuevas of the Nuevo Laredo Owls, as he defeated the Mexico City Reds, 1-0, on August 15, 1953.

RELIEF PITCHING

The first outstanding relief pitcher, or "saver", in the major leagues was Jack Manning of Boston (N.L.) who, in 40 innings of relief in 1876, recorded an ERA of 0.68 with no losses. He also registered 5 saves, a total that was not surpassed for twenty-nine years. Manning's regular position was right field.

Firpo Marberry of the Washington Senators is generally considered to have been the first short-relief specialist of the modern-era. He began relief pitching in 1924, and was followed several years later by others, such as Wilcy Moore of the New York Yankees and Garland Braxton of the Washington Senators.

PITCHING PERFORMANCES

MOST SAVES, SEASON

The all-time record for the most saves in one season is 45 by Dan Quisenberry of the Kansas City Royals. This was accomplished in 69 relief appearances and accounted for 57% of his team's wins in 1983. Bruce Sutter of the St. Louis Cardinals also recorded 45 saves in 1984.

ULTIMATE SHORT-RELIEF PERFORMANCE

On July 27, 1930, Ken Ash of the Cincinnati Reds entered the game against Chicago in the sixth inning with runners on first and third, and no outs. He then proceeded to get the first batter to hit into a triple play. His team scored four runs in the bottom of the sixth and went on to win, 6-5.

LONGEST RELIEF PERFORMANCE

On June 17, 1915, pitcher Zip Zabel of the Chicago Cubs made a relief appearance in the first inning against Brooklyn. He pitched a total of 18 1/3 innings before winning in the nineteenth, 4-3.

FIRST PITCHING MACHINE

In 1897, Professor Charles Hinton of Princeton invented the "Pitching Cannon", baseball's first pitching apparatus. The gun was activated by a spark, using gunpowder to shoot the ball toward the batter.

In a demonstration given on June 10th of that year, the device was used to pitch for both teams in an exhibition game. In three innings it recorded 8 strikeouts, 1 walk, 1 wild pitch and gave up 4 hits. The main complaint was about the long delay required for reloading.

Other early mechanical pitchers were developed by Alexander MacMillan in 1914 and by Dode Paskert in 1916.

AMBIDEXTROUS PLAYERS

Several major league players have had the ability to throw both right and left handed. During the 1880s, four pitchers demonstrated the feat of "switch-pitching" during regular season games.

Tony Mullane of the Louisville Eclipse first pitched using both hands in a 9-8 loss to Baltimore on July 18, 1882. He had developed this technique as an attempt to reduce the strain on his regular pitching arm. Mullane also used this skill with success on pick-off attempts.

Larry Corcoran of Chicago (N.L.) pitched four innings against Buffalo on June 16, 1884, using his right and left hands alternately. His team lost, though, 20-9.

In 1887, the New York Giants signed ambidextrous pitcher John Roach. In his first, and only, game on May 14, he was hit by Philadelphia for seventeen runs and twenty-two hits.

On May 9, 1888, Icebox Chamberlain, a right-handed pitcher for Louisville, defeated Kansas City, 18-6, as he finished the game by pitching the last two innings with his left hand.

Boo Ferriss of the Boston Red Sox (1945-1950) would some times warm-up before games throwing both right and left handed. While in college, at Mississippi State, he performed as a right-handed pitcher and a left-handed first baseman.

Outfielder Edd Roush (1913-1931); catcher Paul Richards (1932-1946); shortstop Bert Campaneris (1964-81,83) and pitcher Jorge Rubio (1966-1967) were also ambidextrous. On August 13, 1962, Campaneris made the last switch-pitching performance in professional ball. As a relief pitcher for Daytona Beach, he threw with both hands in a Florida State League game against Ft. Lauderdale.

BLOOPER PITCH

Rip Sewell, who pitched for the Pittsburgh Pirates between 1938-1949, used an off-speed blooper pitch called the "Eephus Ball". He first threw it in an exhibition game against Detroit on April 10, 1943, and went on to win 21 games that year.

Clark Griffith (1891-1914) and Urban Shocker (1916-1928) had also thrown exaggerated change-ups with some success. Steve Hamilton developed his verson of it, the "Folly Floater", in 1969.

Relief pitcher Dave LaRoche introduced a blooper pitch called "LaLob" in 1980. It was clocked at 28 m.p.h.; the slowest time ever recorded for a pitched ball. On June 30, 1982, LaRoche threw 7 consecutive blooper pitches to Gorman Thomas of Milwaukee.

CHANGE-UP

The change-up, or slow ball, is not actually a specific kind of pitch, but rather a slower version of any number of pitches. A change-up thrown at medium speed has been found to usually be the most effective.

In 1869, ex-cricket bowler Harry Wright of the Cincinnati Red Stockings developed the change-of-pace in an effort to disrupt the batters' timing. It was Tim Keefe, though, who later perfected it. It became his big pitch, interspersing it with his excellent fastball and curve. Keefe pitched from 1880-1893.

PITCHING PERFORMANCES

CURVE BALL

Candy Cummings, who pitched in the old National Association from 1872-1875 and in the National League from 1876-1877, is credited (by most sources) with the invention of the curve ball. In 1867, a public demonstration was given by Cummings in Brooklyn. It was in this demonstration that the theory of the curve being an optical illusion was disproved. Cummings, though, did not use the pitch in a game until many years later, as wrist-snap deliveries were banned at the time.

In a college game between Yale and Harvard on June 14, 1874, Ham Avery of Yale became the first pitcher to throw the curve in an actual game.

Tests have shown that a major league curve ball can break as much as 17 1/2 inches.

EMERY BALL

Russ Ford, who pitched for the New York Yankees and Buffalo Blues (F.L.) from 1909-1915, started a craze with a pitch called the "emery ball". He would wrap a strip of emery paper around a ring on his glove hand, with a small hole cut in his glove to expose the paper. With this he would scuff the ball, causing it to do a series of strange dips, jumps and swerves when thrown.

Similar pitches using scuffed or cut balls were later perfected by Smokey Joe Williams of the Lincoln Giants and Bill Gatewood of the Chicago Giants while playing in the old Negro leagues, and by Whitey Ford of the New York Yankees (1950,53-67).

FORK BALL

The fork ball, held between the index and middle fingers, is thrown with the same motion as a fastball, but breaks downward before reaching the plate. It was developed in the minor leagues by Bun Troy, who later pitched for the Detroit Tigers in 1912.

Joe Bush learned to throw the fork ball in 1920 and led the Yankees to pennants in 1922 and 1923. In the old Eastern Colored League, Red Ryan employed a fork ball to win 20 games and lead Hilldale to the 1923 pennant.

The pitch was also used very successfully by relief pitchers Roy Face (1953-1969) and Lindy McDaniel (1955-1975).

KNUCKLEBALL

The knuckleball, which floats toward the plate and then breaks abruptly a few feet in front of it, has been used by many pitchers, most notably by Hoyt Wilhelm and Phil Niekro.

The first pitcher to throw the knuckleball is said to have been Ed Summers, who pitched for the Detroit Tigers from 1908-1912, leading them to pennants in 1908 and 1909. The first to actually perfect the pitch, though, was Eddie Rommel of the Philadelphia Athletics (1920-1932).

SCREWBALL

The screwball, a curve which breaks in the opposite direction of a regular curve ball, was developed by Mickey Welch, who pitched for the Troy Trojans and New York Giants from 1880-1892.

It was later perfected by Christy Mathewson, who had learned the pitch from teammate Ned Garvin, while playing for Taunton (New England League) in 1899. Rube Foster, Carl Hubbell and Warren Spahn also had great success while throwing the screwball.

PITCHING PERFORMANCES

SHINE BALL

Dave Danforth is credited with originating the "shine ball" in 1915, while pitching for Louisville in the American Association. The groundskeepers at that time used to put oil on the infields to keep down the dust. Danforth found that when he rubbed the ball on his uniform, the combination of oil and dirt would cause the ball to shine on one side. The pitch would appear as a fastball, but would then sail or rise in an unnatural manner. Danforth helped pitch the Chicago White Sox to a World Series victory in 1917.

Eddie Cicotte (1905-1920) and Hod Eller (1917-1921) also used the shine ball until it was banned in 1920.

SLIDER

The slider, which has also been called the short-curve, is a pitch that approaches home plate like a fastball, but then suddenly veers, or slides, a few inches to one side. It breaks just enough to throw the batter off stride.

George Uhle of the Detroit Tigers "discovered" the pitch while playing catch with teammate Harry Heilmann in 1929. He is also credited with naming it.

Several pitchers in the 1930s, including Johnny Babich and George Blaeholder, threw natural sliders. Other early practitioners were Johnny Allen, Al Milnar, Johnny Sain and Mel Parnell.

The slider is a popular pitch today because it is relatively easy to throw and is difficult for the batter to recognize.

SPITBALL

The spitball was first used by Bobby Mathews of the Lord

Baltimores in 1868. He would rub the ball with his hands, keeping one side of it clean, before moistening it with his fingers. His pitches would drop and curve in such a way that no pitchers of his day could duplicate.

The spitball was later discovered, accidently, in 1902 by outfielder George Hildebrand of the Providence Grays (Eastern League). While warming up before a game, he jokingly put a big daub of spit on the ball and threw it. The ball made such a peculiar drop, that teammate Frank Corridon tried it in an exhibition game against Pittsburgh and struck out 9 batters in five innings.

Hildebrand was traded to the Sacramento Senators later that season. It was there that he taught teammate Elmer Stricklett how to throw the "wet ball". Stricklett then won 11 straight games, and later went on to become the second spitball pitcher in the majors.

Spitball has now become the term used to describe any kind of "doctored" baseball.

SUBMARINE PITCH

Prior to 1884, it was required that pitches be delivered in an underhand motion, similar to that used today in fast-pitch softball.

Billy Rhines (1890-1899) brought back a modified version of this delivery when he developed the submarine pitch. He won 28 games in 1890 and 21 in 1897.

The pitch was later made famous by Carl Mays (1915-1929), who learned to throw it while playing for Portland of the Class B Northwestern League in 1913. The submarine pitch has also been used by several pitchers, including Joe McGinnity (1899-1908); Eldon Auker (1933-1942); Dan Quisenberry (1979-1984); and Negro league pitchers Dizzy Dismukes, Webster

McDonald and Scrip Lee. It is also used today by many pitchers in the Japanese leagues.

Chapter Three

FIELDING FEATS

ALL-TIME MAJOR LEAGUE GOLD GLOVE TEAM
(based on career fielding averages)

Pitcher	- Woody Fryman (1966-1983)	.991
Catcher	- Bill Freehan (1961-1976)	.993
1st Base	- Steve Garvey (1969-1984)	.996
2nd Base	- Nellie Fox (1947-1963)	.984
3rd Base	- Brooks Robinson (1955-1977)	.971
Shortstop	- Larry Bowa (1970-1984)	.980
Outfield	- Pete Rose (1963,67-76,78,83-84)	.991
Outfield	- Joe Rudi (1968-1982)	.991
Outfield	- Mickey Stanley (1964-1978)	.991

MOST PUTOUTS, LIFETIME

The most putouts by one player in the major leagues is 23,696 by first baseman Jake Beckley. He played for five different teams between 1888-1907 and led the league in putouts six times during his career.

MOST PUTOUTS, SEASON

The record for the most putouts in one season was set in 1905 by first baseman and manager Pop Dillon of the league champion Los Angeles Angels (Pacific Coast League). He registered 2,242 putouts that year.

First baseman Jiggs Donahue of the Chicago White Sox recorded 1,846 putouts in 1907 to set the major league record, breaking his own mark of 1,697 set the year before. He also led the major leagues in fielding pct. in 1907.

MOST PUTOUTS, GAME

The greatest number of putouts in a nine-inning major league game is 22. The mark was originally set by first baseman Tom Jones of the St. Louis Browns during an 8-3 victory over Boston on May 11, 1906. Hal Chase of New York tied the record later that season, on September 21. It was also duplicated by Ernie Banks of the Chicago Cubs on May 9, 1963 in a game against Pittsburgh.

First baseman Walter Holke of the Boston Braves recorded the all-time high of 42 putouts in the record 26-inning game against Brooklyn on May 1, 1920.

MOST ASSISTS, LIFETIME

Shortstop Luis Aparicio registered 8,016 assists in his career to set the major league record. He played for the Chicago White Sox, Baltimore Orioles and Boston Red Sox between 1956-1973 and led the league in assists seven times. He also won eight Gold Glove Awards, the most ever by a shortstop.

MOST ASSISTS, SEASON

The all-time record for assists in one season is 807 by second baseman George Cutshaw, who played for the Oakland Oaks of the Pacific Coast League in 1910. He later went on to lead the National League four times in this category.

Second baseman Frankie Frisch of the St. Louis Cardinals set the major league record of 641 assists in 1927. He also led all second basemen in fielding pct. that year.

FIELDING FEATS

MOST ASSISTS, GAME

The major league record for the most assists in a nine-inning game is 14 by shortstop Tommy Corcoran of the Cincinnati Reds. It was established in a 4-2 victory over St. Louis on August 7, 1903.

Lave Cross of the Philadelphia Phillies recorded 15 assists in a 12-inning game against New York on August 5, 1897. Shortstop Rick Burleson of the California Angels also recorded 15 assists on April 13, 1982 in a 20-inning game against Seattle.

FEWEST CHANCES ACCEPTED, GAME

Six major league first basemen have accomplished the rare feat of going through an entire game without fielding a single ball:

Guy Hecker, Louisville (A.A.), October 9, 1887
Al McCauley, Washington (A.A.), August 6, 1891
Bud Clancy, Chicago (A.L.), April 27, 1930
Rip Collins, Chicago (N.L.), June 29, 1937
Norm Cash, Detroit (A.L.), June 27, 1963
Gene Tenace, Oakland (A.L.), September 1, 1974

MOST DOUBLE PLAYS, LIFETIME

Mickey Vernon, who played first base for six different clubs between 1939-1960, holds the major league record for being involved in 2,044 double plays. During his career, he led the American League in double plays three times.

MOST DOUBLE PLAYS, SEASON

First baseman Ferris Fain of the Philadelphia Athletics

47

took part in 194 double plays in 1949, shattering the old mark of 163. In two consecutive seasons, he was involved in a total of 386 double plays.

MOST DOUBLE PLAYS, GAME

The record for the most double plays in one major league game is 7, accomplished by first baseman Curt Blefary of the Houston Astros in a game against San Francisco on May 4, 1969. Normally an outfielder, this was the only season that he played first base on a regular basis. Houston won the game, 3-1.

This performance equaled the professional record which had been established by first baseman Jack Burns of the Wichita Falls Spudders. On June 6, 1930, Burns had taken part in 7 double plays during a Class A Texas League game against Waco.

MOST UNASSISTED DOUBLE PLAYS, GAME

The major league record for the most unassisted double plays in one game is 2. Excluding first basemen, there have been just four players who have performed this feat:

Davy Force, Buffalo (N.L.), September 15, 1881
Claude Ritchey, Louisville (N.L.), July 9, 1899
Lee Tannehill, Chicago (A.L.), August 4, 1911
Mike Edwards, Oakland (A.L.), August 10, 1978

FIRST UNASSISTED TRIPLE PLAY

The ultimate fielding performance, the unassisted triple play, was first performed by Hal O'Hagan, a first baseman for the Rochester Bronchos, in an International League game against Jersey City on August 18, 1902. After catching a bunt that had been popped up, he doubled the runner off first and then ran to second before the other runner returned.

For many years, it was believed that Paul Hines of the Providence Grays made the first unassisted triple play in 1878. He had actually performed an unassisted double play, with an assist on the third out, in a game against Boston. It was a triple play, but not unassisted.

QUADRUPLE PLAY

The only instance of a quadruple play was by the New York Giants in a game against St. Louis on July 1, 1903. In the sixth inning, the Cardinals loaded the bases with no outs. The next batter hit a fly ball to Roger Bresnahan in center field (1 out), whose throw to home nailed the runner trying to score (2 outs). The runner on first had made a delayed attempt to reach second, but was thrown out by catcher John Warner (3 outs). The return throw by George Davis to Warner caught the confused runner from second, who had rounded third and was attempting to score (4 outs). New York went on to win the game, 5-2.

Though the final out, of course, did not count, it, nevertheless, demonstrates that a quadruple play can be performed.

MOST ERRORS, SEASON

The greatest number of errors committed by a major league player in one season is 115. This was accomplished by shortstop Bill Shindle, while playing for the Philadelphia Quakers of the Players' League in 1890. Since then, only one other player has been charged with 100 or more errors (Joe Sullivan in 1893), as the introduction of gloves greatly improved infield play.

The minor league record since 1900 was set by shortstop Russ Hall of the Seattle Siwashes (Pacific Coast League) when he committed 119 errors during the 1904 season.

FIELDING FEATS

FEWEST ERRORS, SEASON

Admittedly, some positions are required to field a consid-
erably greater number of difficult chances than others. There
have been major league players at the following positions who
have gone through an entire season (100 games minimum for
non-pitchers) without committing an error: pitcher, catcher,
first base, left field, center field and right field.

The last player to record a fielding pct. of 1.000 was
first baseman Steve Garvey of the San Diego Padres in 1984.

MOST ERRORS, GAME

Andy Leonard, Irish-born second baseman for Boston (N.L.),
set a major league record (pre-glove era) by committing 9 errors
in a game against St. Louis on June 14, 1876. Normally an
outfielder, he occasionally filled in at second base that
season. This contest, which featured a total of 41 errors by
both teams, has been called the worst played game in major
league history. St. Louis won, 20-6, although only five of
their runs were earned.

Since 1900, the major league record of 5 errors is held by
seven different players. It was last performed by second
baseman Nap Lajoie of the Philadelphia Athletics on April 22,
1915 in a 7-6 loss to Boston.

MOST ERRORS, INNING

The major league record for the most errors in one inning
is 4, held by the following:

Shorty Fuller, Washington (N.L.), August 17, 1888
Lew Whistler, New York (N.L.), June 19, 1891
Doggie Miller, St. Louis (N.L.), May 24, 1895
Jimmy Burke, Milwaukee (A.L.), May 27, 1901

FIELDING FEATS

Ray Chapman, Cleveland (A.L.), June 20, 1914
Lennie Merullo, Chicago (N.L.), September 13, 1942

MOST POSITIONS, GAME

Since 1900, there have been six major leaguers who have played all nine positions in one season. Two of those played nine positions in one game.

On September 8, 1965, Bert Campaneris played each position for the Kansas City Athletics in a game against California. Starting at shortstop, he played a different position each inning. He pitched in the eighth, and allowed one run. Kansas City lost, though, 5-3.

Cesar Tovar of the Minnesota Twins duplicated this feat on September 22, 1968 in a game against Oakland. He pitched a hitless first inning, and then went on to play an inning at each of the other eight positions. Minnesota won, 2-1.

This has also been accomplished several times in the minor leagues and, in fact, was once performed by nine players in one game. In a Class A Northwest League game on August 31, 1974, manager Frank Peters of the Portland Mavericks rotated his players so that each played one inning at a different position against Tri-Cities. Portland won the game, 8-7. The players were Reggie Thomas, Cliff Holland, Ed Cervantes, Bobby Waits, Dave Falkosky, Ron Weyand, Sanford Sigman, Mike Uremovich and Jim Emery.

Mike Ashman of the Albany-Colonie A's set a record on September 3, 1983 by playing 10 positions in an Eastern League game against Nashua. Starting the game as the DH, he then switched to left field in the first inning, and proceeded to play a different position each inning. His team won the game, 5-3.

51

FIELDING FEATS

DEFENSIVE SHIFTS

The first recorded instance of an exaggerated shift was in the pre-1910 era, when Chicago used a shift designed to defense the hitting of Mike Donlin of the New York Giants.

On July 14, 1946, in a game against Boston, manager Lou Boudreau of the Cleveland Indians instituted the famous "Williams Shift". This was an attempt to curb the hitting of pull-hitting slugger Ted Williams. Cleveland swung its defensive line-up to the right, as Williams rarely hit to left field.

Williams beat the shift on September 13, 1946, when he hit a ball to unoccupied left field that went for an inside-the-park home run. This shift was similar to the one employed by National League teams in the 1920s against power hitting Cy Williams of the Philadelphia Phillies.

Probably the most exaggerated shift in baseball was that used by the Hiroshima Carp on May 5, 1964 against Sadaharu Oh of the Yomiuri Giants. In this alignment all of the fielders were moved to right and center field, leaving the entire left side empty.

FIVE-MAN INFIELD

Another unique defensive shift was the "five-man infield", which was devised by Branch Rickey and first used by the Brooklyn Dodgers in 1950.

When the team at bat has the winning run on third base in the ninth inning with less than two outs, an outfielder is brought in as the fifth man in the infield. The first and third basemen then move to within twenty feet from the batter. The idea is to force the batter to swing away, either striking out or grounding to one of the infielders. The five-man infield is still occasionally used in the majors, most recently by the Pittsburgh Pirates and Philadelphia Phillies in 1984.

FIELDING FEATS

UNGLAUB'S ARC

In 1907, first baseman Bob Unglaub of the Boston Red Sox devised a way to improve the hitting and create more excitement in the game during the dead-ball era. He suggested that an arc, 240 feet from home plate, be drawn across the outfield. Outfielders would then be required to position themselves within the line until the ball was hit.

Though this concept was briefly considered, it was never adopted for use in professional ball.

RECORD ALTITUDE CATCHES

800 FEET

On April 1, 1930, catcher Gabby Hartnett of the Chicago Cubs set an all-time record for "altitude catches". He caught the ball dropped from a blimp, an estimated 800 feet above the ground, prior to an exhibition game at Wrigley Field in Los Angeles.

Joe Sprinz, a catcher for the San Francisco Seals of the Pacific Coast League, made an attempt to duplicate this record on August 3, 1939. He momentarily held onto the ball, which was traveling at almost 150 m.p.h. But, the tremendous force pushed the glove into his face, knocking out five teeth, breaking his jaw and causing him to drop the ball.

700 FEET

On August 20, 1938, Cleveland catchers Hank Helf and Frankie Pytlak each caught balls dropped from the upper ledge of the 52-story Cleveland Terminal Tower, a distance of 708 feet. The velocity was estimated at 138 m.p.h.

Outfielder Mike Zarefoos of the Cleveland Competitors (North American Softball League) matched this record when he caught a softball dropped from the Cleveland Terminal Tower on June 24, 1980.

FIELDING FEATS

600 FEET

At State-Line Airpark in Kansas City on October 17, 1954, Bobo Nickerson of the House of David team caught a ball dropped from an airplane at 650 feet.

500 FEET

Catcher Dutch Dotterer of the Cincinnati Reds caught a ball dropped from a helicopter at Cosley Field in August, 1954. The ball traveled 575 feet.

On August 25, 1894, catcher Pop Schriver of Chicago (N.L.) attempted to catch a ball dropped from the observation deck of the Washington Monument, a distance of 504 feet. There are conflicting reports, though, on whether he actually made the catch. Buck Ewing, Paul Hines and Pop Snyder had each failed on separate occasions to accomplish this feat.

Gabby Street, a catcher for the Washington Senators, is credited by most sources as having been the first player to catch a ball dropped from the Washington Monument on August 21, 1908. It has been estimated that a ball dropped from that height reaches a speed of almost 120 m.p.h. Two years later, on August 24, 1910, Billy Sullivan of the Chicago White Sox duplicated this feat.

400 FEET

On May 11, 1925, Chicago White Sox catcher Ray Schalk caught a ball dropped from the tower of the Chicago Tribune Building. The ball traveled a distance of 460 feet.

On April 6, 1944, outfielder Danny Gardella and first baseman Phil Weintraub of the New York Giants each caught balls dropped from a blimp, 400 feet above the ground, prior to an exhibition game against Jersey City in Lakehurst, New Jersey.

300 FEET

Kurt Bevacqua of the San Diego Padres caught five consecutive baseballs dropped from the roof of the new Imperial Bank

Building in San Diego in September, 1982. The balls traveled 390 feet and reached a speed of 110 m.p.h.

Babe Ruth became the first player to catch a ball dropped from an airplane on July 22, 1926. He caught the ball from a height of 300 feet at Mitchell Field in New York.

SINISTRAL SECOND BASEMEN

The most difficult position for a left-handed fielder is that of a second baseman. The main reason is that the ball cannot be fielded in an adequate throwing position, particularly in double play situations after the force-out at second. However, several left-handers have actually played second base as their regular position.

In 1871, Al Reach of the Philadelphia Athletics became the first in professional ball. During the 1880s, second basemen Bill Greenwood and Bill McClellan were also left-handed. Greenwood had the highest fielding average among American Association second basemen in 1887.

5'4-1/2" Kid Mohler played twenty-five seasons in the minor leagues (1890-1914) at second base.

SINISTRAL CATCHERS

Another baseball rarity is the left-handed catcher. This is due more to tradition, though, than to any great disadvantage on the part of a left-hander.

The first southpaw to play this position in professional baseball was Fergy Malone of the champion Philadelphia Athletics in 1871. Other left-handed catchers were Jack Clements (1884-1900) and Pop Tate (1885-1890). Clements' other distinction was that he was also one of the first major league players to have worn a chest protector.

FIELDING FEATS

The last lefty to play catcher in a major league game was Mike Squires of the Chicago White Sox. Normally a first baseman, he caught the last few innings in a game against Kansas City on May 7, 1980.

LONGEST BASEBALL THROW

The longest measured baseball throw is 445'10" by Canadian-born outfielder Glen Gorbous of the Omaha Cardinals (American Association) on August 1, 1957.

Evolution of the Longest Throw Record

400'7-1/2"	John Hatfield, New York (N.A.), October 15, 1872
416'7-3/4"	Tony Mullane, Detroit (N.L.), 1881
426'9-1/2"	Larry LeJeune, Evansville (C.L.), October 9, 1910
434'1"	Don Grate, Chattanooga (S.A.), September 7, 1952
443'3-1/2"	Don Grate, Chattanooga (S.A.), August 23, 1953
445'10"	Glen Gorbous, Omaha (A.A.), August 1, 1957

In comparison, the record throw for a heavier cricket ball (5-1/2 oz.) is 422 feet. This was accomplished by Robert Percival of England on April 18, 1881.

LONGEST BASEBALL THROW, WOMEN'S RECORD

The women's record for the longest baseball throw is 296 feet by Babe Didrickson of Dallas on July 25, 1931. This effort broke her own record of 268'10" set the year before. Didrickson won two gold medals in the 1932 Olympics and also pitched in exhibition games for the Phhiladelphia Athletics and St. Louis Cardinals in 1934.

Lizzie Arnold of Seattle had a throw of 209'5" on October 18, 1909, and is believed to be the first woman to have broken the two-hundred foot mark.

FIELDING FEATS

Evolution of the Women's Throwing Record

224'2-1/4"	Eleanore Churchill, Exeter, N.H., September 16, 1922
234'5-3/4"	Eleanore Churchill, Exeter, N.H., September 29, 1923
256'0"	Vivian Hardwick, Pasadena, California, 1928
258'1"	Gloria Russell, Eureka, California, July 27, 1929
268'10"	Babe Didrickson, Dallas, Texas, July 4, 1930
296'0"	Babe Didrickson, Dallas, Texas, July 25, 1931

FIRST GLOVES

The first player to wear a glove during a game is believed to have been Doug Allison, a catcher for Cincinnati in 1869. He had suffered an injury to the palm of his hand, and since his team had no other catchers, he was needed to continue playing. He cut the fingers off of a regular hand glove and used it to protect his injured hand.

In 1875, first baseman Charlie Waitt of St. Louis wore a flesh-colored buckskin glove to protect his catching hand during a National Association game against Boston. Two years later, pitcher Al Spalding of Chicago introduced a padded glove.

In the 1880s, Henry Fabian of New Orleans and Silver Flint of Chicago became the first catchers to use padded gloves. Catcher Buck Ewing of the New York Giants later developed the first pillow-type mitt in 1890.

By the 1890s, all major leaguers had adopted the use of gloves in the field. Second baseman Bid McPhee of the Cincinnati Reds, the last bare-handed fielder, wore one for the first time in 1896.

Many of the later innovations of baseball gloves were credited to Bud Latina, a former minor league player who joined the Rawlings Sporting Goods Company in 1922.

Birdie Tebbetts, who played catcher for three different teams between 1936-1952, was the first player to wear a golf glove while batting.

FIELDING FEATS

FIRST CATCHER'S MASK

Fred Thayer, third baseman and captain of the Harvard University team, invented the catcher's mask. He employed a tinsmith to construct it, using a fencing mask as the model. The mask was first worn by Harvard catcher Jim Tyng in an exhibition game against Boston (N.L.) on April 12, 1877, and was adopted soon after by the professionals.

Before the invention of the catcher's mask, a rubber mouth protector was used by those who played the position.

FIRST SHIN GUARDS

Second baseman Bud Fowler, the first black professional player in 1872, is credited with the invention of the shin guards. To keep from getting spiked, he played with the lower part of his legs encased in wooden guards.

In 1906, Red Dooin of the Philadelphia Phillies became the first major league catcher to wear shin guards in a game. These pads, similar to those worn by college football players at that time, were concealed underneath his socks.

Roger Bresnahan of the New York Giants introduced heavier-padded shin guards a a means of protection. These were patterned after those worn by wicket keepers (catchers) in cricket. He wore them for the first time on April 11, 1907 in a game against Philadelphia.

Chapter Four

RUNNING RECORDS

MOST RUNS SCORED, LIFETIME

Spencer Harris, who played for ten different teams during his 26-year minor league career (1921-1948), holds the record for scoring 2,287 runs. He is one of only three players who reached the 2,000 mark in the minor leagues. (Source: Minor League Baseball Stars, SABR)

The major league record for the most runs scored is 2,244 by Ty Cobb, who played for the Detroit Tigers and Philadelphia Athletics between 1905-1928. He also led the American League in scoring five times during his career.

MOST RUNS SCORED, SEASON

Back in baseball's early days, shortstop George Wright of the champion Cincinnati Red Stockings was credited with scoring a total of 339 runs in 1869. Tony Lazzeri, shortstop for the Salt Lake City Bees of the Pacific Coast League, set the professional league record when he scored 202 runs in 1925 (197 games).

Five-foot-six-inch center-fielder Billy Hamilton of the Philadelphia Phillies scored 196 runs in 1894, a major league record (129 games). He also established another mark by scoring a run in 24 consecutive games that year.

FIRST RUN

The first run ever scored in a professional league game was

by catcher Bill Lennon of the Fort Wayne Kekiongas in the National Association opener against Cleveland on May 4, 1871. He scored from second on teammate Joe McDermott's single in the second inning.

Catcher Tim McGinley of Boston had the distinction of scoring the first major league run. This occurred on April 22, 1876 against Philadelphia in the National League's inaugural game.

ONE-MILLIONTH RUN

First baseman Bob Watson of the Houston Astros scored major league run No. 1,000,000 on May 4, 1975, as he crossed the plate in the second inning of a game against San Francisco. For his efforts, he received a $1,000 watch. His shoes and home plate were sent to the Hall of Fame.

MOST STOLEN BASES, LIFETIME

The all-time record for the most stolen bases is 1,010 by Yutaka Fukumoto of the Hankyu Braves. A five-foot-seven-inch center-fielder, he has played in the Japanese Pacific League from 1969-1984.

The minor league mark is 948 by George Hogriever, who played for thirteen different teams between 1889-1912. (Source: Minor League Baseball Stars, SABR)

In nineteen seasons with the Chicago Cubs and St. Louis Cardinals (1961-1979), Lou Brock established the major league record of 938 stolen bases. He also led the majors six times during his career.

In major league history, there have been fifteen players who have stolen 600 or more bases in their careers. It should be noted that prior to 1898 stolen bases were credited any time a runner advanced an extra base on a hit or out. Since these bases advanced cannot be separated from bases stolen, according to the modern definition, totals from this era are not usually recognized.

MOST STOLEN BASES, SEASON (since 1900)

(Major league players - CAPITALIZED)

145	Vince Coleman, Macon, 1983
144	Donnell Nixon, Bakersfield, 1983
130	RICKEY HENDERSON, OAKLAND, 1982
124	Jimmy Johnston, San Francisco, 1913
123	Jeff Stone, Spartanburg, 1981
120	Allan Wiggins, Lodi, 1980
118	LOU BROCK, ST. LOUIS, 1974
116	Ralph Myers, Spokane, 1912
116	Allan Lewis, Leesburg, 1966
111	Ovid Nicholson, Frankfurt, 1912

In the old Negro leagues, outfielder Cool Papa Bell of the Pittsburgh Crawfords stole a record 175 bases in 1933 (approx. 200 games).

Yutaka Fukumoto of the Hankyu Braves established the Japanese League record of 106 stolen bases in 1972 (122 games).

MOST STOLEN BASES, CONSECUTIVE

The major league record for the most consecutive stolen bases is 38 by Davey Lopes of the Los Angeles Dodgers in 1975. He also went on to lead the majors in steals that year with 77.

RUNNING RECORDS

MOST STOLEN BASES, GAME

Center-fielder George Gore of Chicago, the N.L. champions, set the major league (pre-1900) record when he stole 7 bases in a game against Providence on June 25, 1881. The record was tied by Billy Hamilton of the Philadelphia Phillies in the second game of doubleheader against Washington on August 31, 1894.

Fred Werber of the Augusta Tygers set the minor league record when he stole 7 bases in a South Atlantic League game on June 11, 1927. This record was later equaled by Lee Mazzilli of the Visalia Oaks on June 8, 1975 and by Rickey Henderson of the Modesto A's on May 26, 1977. Both took place in the Class A California League.

In the Mexican League, second baseman Antonio Briones of the Juarez Indians stole 7 bases on June 2, 1980 in a game against Poza Rica.

BASE STEALING SWEEPS

Since 1900, there have been thirty-two instances in major league history when a player has stolen his way around the bases. It was first achieved by Dave Fultz, a center-fielder for the Philadelphia Athletics, on September 4, 1902 against Detroit. The last player to perform this feat was Dusty Baker of the San Francisco Giants on June 27, 1984 in the third inning of a 14-9 victory over Cincinnati.

Ty Cobb and Honus Wagner both performed the base-stealing hat trick 3 times during their careers.

There has been one occasion in baseball history when a player has stolen 4 bases in one time at bat. This occurred on May 5, 1956 in a game between two Washington colleges. Don Jacobs of Olympic College stole second against Skagit Valley College, but thinking that the batter had fouled off the pitch, he returned to first. He then proceeded to steal second, third and home, and was credited with four steals by the official scorer.

FIRST SLIDE

Ned Cuthbert, an outfielder for the Philadelphia Keystones, is generally credited with having performed the first slide. This took place in a game against the Brooklyn Atlantics in 1865, as he slid into third with the first stolen base.

The slide was considered a circus stunt and created considerable excitement at the time.

CIRCLING THE BASES

The fastest recorded time for a player to circle the bases is 13.3 seconds. This was established in a pre-game race by outfielder Evar Swanson of the Columbus Redbirds (American Association) on September 20, 1931.

The major league record is also held by Swanson. On September 15, 1929, he circled the bases in 13.4 seconds while he was a member of the Cincinnati Reds. He had previously played several seasons as an end in the N.F.L. (1924-1927).

Evolution of Record for Circling Bases

14.0 Billy Sunday, Chicago (N.L.), 1887
13.8 Hans Lobert, Cincinnati (N.L.), 1910
13.6 Maurice Archdeacon, Rochester (I.L.), 1921
13.4 Evar Swanson, Cincinnati (N.L.), 1929
13.3 Evar Swanson, Columbus (A.A.), 1931

The closest that anyone has come to Swanson's record is 13.4 by Maury Wills of the Miami Sun Sox (Class B Florida

International League) in 1953. George Case of the Washington Senators (1943) and Cliff McClain, University of California (1948), were both timed in 13.5 seconds.

Unsubstantiated reports of sub-thirteen second runs have been attributed to Negro league outfielder Cool Papa Bell and early-1900 professional sprinter R.P. Williams.

WRONG-WAY RUNNERS

The first instance of a wrong-way runner in baseball reportedly took place in a spring exhibition game on April 25, 1883, as outfielder Dan O'Leary of Port Huron hit a home run against the Peoria Reds of the old Northwestern League. It is claimed that after crossing home plate, he was called out by the umpire. Apparently, he had fallen down, somehow lost his sense of direction (?) and run around the bases the wrong way.

On April 27, 1902, Jim St. Vrain, a rookie pitcher for the Chicago Cubs, also made the mistake of running the wrong way. He was a right-handed hitter, but at the request of his manager, he attempted to bat left-handed in a game against Pittsburgh. After hitting a grounder to the shortstop, he got confused and ran toward third base. The startled shortstop, Honus Wagner, threw to first for the out. Pittsburgh went on to win the game, 2-0.

First baseman Harry Davis of the Philadelphia Athletics, in a game against Detroit in 1902, singled, stole second and then shocked everyone by returning to first base on the next pitch. In the confusion, the runner on third scored. Germany Schaefer of the Washington Senators duplicated this same play in the ninth inning of a game against Chicago on August 4, 1911.

Catcher Eddy "New" Deal of the House of David team, when on third base, would occasionally create excitement by going back and stealing second. The rules were later changed to prohibit a player from intentionally running the bases in reverse order.

RUNNING RECORDS

In 1944, Ray Dumont, president of the National Baseball
Congress (semi-pro ball), devised "razzle-dazzle baseball",
which allows base running in reverse. In this confusing version
of the game, the batter has the option of running either to
first or third base. Runners then have to continue in the
direction they started. A total of up to two men are allowed on
each base.

ATTEMPTED STEAL OF AN OCCUPIED BASE

Probably the most embarrassing play that a baserunner can
make, besides running the wrong way, is attempting to steal a
base which a teammate is already occupying.

In a 1904 game against St. Louis, outfielder John Anderson
of New York (A.L.) broke from first and slid into second with an
apparent steal. However, the bases were already full.

Among the others who have performed a "bone-head steal" are
Ty Cobb, Beals Becker, Grover Cleveland Alexander, Goose Goslin
and Babe Herman. Red Faber once attempted to steal an occupied
base in the second game of the 1917 World Series.

There has been one instance when this play has worked to
the advantage of the baserunner. On June 21, 1917, Red McKee of
the San Francisco Seals attempted to steal third with the bases
loaded in a Pacific Coast League game against Salt Lake City.
He got away with it when the umpire called a balk on the
pitcher.

CUTTING BASES

Before 1911, games were officiated by only one umpire.
Under these circumstances it was extremely difficult for the
umpire to observe everything that occurred during the game.
Occasionally, a player would go from first to third without

touching second or from second to home, running three feet inside of third to cut down the distance to home.

In the 1880s, King Kelly became so adept at this that he sometimes went directly from first to third, cutting across the diamond behind the pitcher's mound.

FASTEST RUNNER IN BASEBALL HISTORY

Baseball has had many outstanding "sprinters" in its long history. This list has included such names as Louis Sockalexis, Hans Lobert, Harry Bay, Jim Thorpe, Evar Swanson, Cool Papa Bell, George Case and Sam Jethroe. Among the fastest players today are Vince Coleman, Rickey Henderson, Tim Raines and Willie Wilson.

The fastest runner in major league history, though, was Herb Washington, a pinch-runner for the Oakland Athletics from 1974-1975. In college, at Michigan State, he set world records of 5.0 seconds in the 50 yard dash and 5.8 seconds in the 60 yard dash. He also had a best time in the 100 of 9.2 seconds.

Chapter Five

TEAM TOTALS

MAJOR LEAGUE CHAMPIONS

	National League	American League	World Series	
1984	San Diego	Detroit	Detroit	4-1
1983	Philadelphia	Baltimore	Baltimore	4-1
1982	St. Louis	Milwaukee	St. Louis	4-3
1981	Los Angeles	New York	Los Angeles	4-2
1980	Philadelphia	Kansas City	Philadelphia	4-2
1979	Pittsburgh	Baltimore	Pittsburgh	4-3
1978	Los Angeles	New York	New York	4-2
1977	Los Angeles	New York	New York	4-2
1976	Cincinnati	New York	Cincinnati	4-0
1975	Cincinnati	Boston	Cincinnati	4-3
1974	Los Angeles	Oakland	Oakland	4-1
1973	New York	Oakland	Oakland	4-3
1972	Cincinnati	Oakland	Oakland	4-3
1971	Pittsburgh	Baltimore	Pittsburgh	4-3
1970	Cincinnati	Baltimore	Baltimore	4-1
1969	New York	Baltimore	New York	4-1
1968	St. Louis	Detroit	Detroit	4-3
1967	St. Louis	Boston	St. Louis	4-3
1966	Los Angeles	Baltimore	Baltimore	4-0
1965	Los Angeles	Minnesota	Los Angeles	4-3
1964	St. Louis	New York	St. Louis	4-3
1963	Los Angeles	New York	Los Angeles	4-0
1962	San Francisco	New York	New York	4-3
1961	Cincinnati	New York	New York	4-1
1960	Pittsburgh	New York	Pittsburgh	4-3
1959	Los Angeles	Chicago	Los Angeles	4-2

TEAM TOTALS

	National League	American League	World Series	
1958	Milwaukee	New York	New York	4-3
1957	Milwaukee	New York	Milwaukee	4-3
1956	Brooklyn	New York	New York	4-3
1955	Brooklyn	New York	Brooklyn	4-3
1954	New York	Cleveland	New York	4-0
1953	Brooklyn	New York	New York	4-2
1952	Brooklyn	New York	New York	4-3
1951	New York	New York	New York AL	4-2
1950	Philadelphia	New York	New York	4-0
1949	Brooklyn	New York	New York	4-1
1948	Boston	Cleveland	Cleveland	4-2
1947	Brooklyn	New York	New York	4-3
1946	St. Louis	Boston	St. Louis	4-3
1945	Chicago	Detroit	Detroit	4-3
1944	St. Louis	St. Louis	St. Louis NL	4-2
1943	St. Louis	New York	New York	4-1
1942	St. Louis	New York	St. Louis	4-1
1941	Brooklyn	New York	New York	4-1
1940	Cincinnati	Detroit	Cincinnati	4-3
1939	Cincinnati	New York	New York	4-0
1938	Chicago	New York	New York	4-0
1937	New York	New York	New York AL	4-1
1936	New York	New York	New York AL	4-2
1935	Chicago	Detroit	Detroit	4-2
1934	St. Louis	Detroit	St. Louis	4-3
1933	New York	Washington	New York	4-1
1932	Chicago	New York	New York	4-0
1931	St. Louis	Philadelphia	St. Louis	4-3
1930	St. Louis	Philadelphia	Philadelphia	4-2
1929	Chicago	Philadelphia	Philadelphia	4-1
1928	St. Louis	New York	New York	4-0
1927	Pittsburgh	New York	New York	4-0
1926	St. Louis	New York	St. Louis	4-3
1925	Pittsburgh	Washington	Pittsburgh	4-3
1924	New York	Washington	Washington	4-3

TEAM TOTALS

	National League	American League	World Series	
1923	New York	New York	New York AL	4-2
1922	New York	New York	New York NL	4-0
1921	New York	New York	New York NL	5-3
1920	Brooklyn	Cleveland	Cleveland	5-2
1919	Cincinnati	Chicago	Cincinnati	5-3
1918	Chicago	Boston	Boston	4-2
1917	New York	Chicago	Chicago	4-2
1916	Brooklyn	Boston	Boston	4-1
1915	Philadelphia	Boston	Boston	4-1
1914	Boston	Philadelphia	Boston	4-0
1913	New York	Philadelphia	Philadelphia	4-1
1912	New York	Boston	Boston	4-3
1911	New York	Philadelphia	Philadelphia	4-2
1910	Chicago	Philadelphia	Philadelphia	4-1
1909	Pittsburgh	Detroit	Pittsburgh	4-3
1908	Chicago	Detroit	Chicago	4-1
1907	Chicago	Detroit	Chicago	4-0
1906	Chicago	Chicago	Chicago AL	4-2
1905	New York	Philadelphia	New York	4-1
1904	New York	Boston	No Series	
1903	Pittsburgh	Boston	Boston	5-3
1902	Pittsburgh	Philadelphia	No Series	
1901	Pittsburgh	Chicago	No Series	
1900	Brooklyn			
1899	Brooklyn			
1898	Boston			

From 1894 through 1897, Series was known as the Temple Cup and played between 1st and 2nd place National League teams.

	National League	American League	World Series	
1897	Boston	Baltimore	Baltimore	4-1
1896	Baltimore	Cleveland	Baltimore	4-0
1895	Baltimore	Cleveland	Cleveland	4-1
1894	Baltimore	New York	New York	4-0
1893	Boston	Pittsburgh	No Series	
1892	Boston	Cleveland	Boston	5-0

69

TEAM TOTALS

	National League	American Assoc.	World Series	
1891	Boston	Boston	No Series	
1890	Brooklyn	Louisville	Tie	3-3
1889	New York	Brooklyn	New York	6-3
1888	New York	St. Louis	New York	6-4
1887	Detroit	St. Louis	Detroit	10-5
1886	Chicago	St. Louis	St. Louis	4-2
1885	Chicago	St. Louis	Tie	3-3
1884	Providence	New York	Providence	3-0
1883	Boston	Philadelphia	No Series	
1882	Chicago	Cincinnati	Tie	1-1
1881	Chicago			
1880	Chicago			
1879	Providence			
1878	Boston			
1877	Boston			
1876	Chicago			

National Association

1875	Boston
1874	Boston
1873	Boston
1872	Boston
1871	Philadelphia

National Association of Base Ball Players

1870	Brooklyn Atlantics
1869	Cincinnati Red Stockings
1868	Philadelphia Athletics
1867	Morrisania Unions
1866	Philadelphia Athletics
1865	Brooklyn Atlantics
1864	Brooklyn Atlantics
1863	Brooklyn Eckfords
1862	Brooklyn Eckfords
1861	Brooklyn

TEAM TOTALS

1860   Undecided
1858-59 New York

Other Major Leagues:

Federal League

1915   Chicago Whales
1914   Indianapolis Hoosiers

Players' League

1890   Boston Beaneaters

Union Association

1884   St. Louis Maroons

MOST PENNANTS (since 1900)

33	New York Yankees (A.L.)
18	Brooklyn/Los Angeles Dodgers (N.L.)
16	New York/San Francisco Giants (N.L.)
13	St. Louis Cardinals (N.L.)
12	Philadelphia/Oakland Athletics (A.L.)
10	Chicago Cubs (N.L.)
9	Boston Red Sox (A.L.)
9	Detroit Tigers (A.L.)
9	Pittsburgh Pirates (N.L.)
8	Cincinnati Reds (N.L.)

BASEBALL DYNASTIES - CONSECUTIVE PENNANTS

Japanese League	- 9	Yomiuri Giants (1965-73)
Minor League	- 7	Baltimore Orioles (1919-25)
Negro League	- 6	Homestead Grays (1940-45)
Major League	- 5	New York Yankees (1949-53 & 1960-64)

MOST WINS, SEASON

116	Chicago Cubs (N.L.), 1906
111	Cleveland Indians (A.L.), 1954
110	Pittsburgh Pirates (N.L.), 1909*
110	New York Yankees (A.L.), 1927*
109	New York Yankees (A.L.), 1961*
109	Baltimore Orioles (A.L.), 1969
108	Baltimore Orioles (A.L.), 1970*
108	Cincinnati Reds (N.L.), 1975*
107	Chicago Cubs (N.L.), 1907*
107	Philadelphia Athletics (A.L.), 1931
107	New York Yankees (A.L.), 1932*

* Won the World Series

The Homestead Grays won 153 games in 1937 en route to the Negro National League pennant. This total included a large number of exhibition game victories, as it was the practice of the owners to schedule as many games each season as possible. Three years earlier, the barnstorming House of David team had recorded a total of 142 victories.

The minor league record was set by the Los Angeles Angels of the Pacific Coast League when they won 137 games during the 1934 season. Their record was 137-50.

MOST WINS, CONSECUTIVE

Early black teams, competing as independents, often compiled impressive winning streaks. The Chicago Leland Giants once won 48 consecutive games in 1907, while the Homestead Grays, in 1926, put together a streak of 43 consecutive victories.

The Cincinnati Red Stockings, the first professional baseball team, won 39 consecutive games in 1869 before being held to a controversial 17-17 tie by the Troy Haymakers on

August 27th. They then went on to finish the season by winning their final eighteen games.

The minor league record is 27 by the Corsicana Oil City of the Texas League in 1902. In the International League the 1921 Baltimore Orioles also won 27 straight on their way to their third consecutive pennant.

The major league record for the most consecutive victories is 26 by the New York Giants in 1916. During this streak, they defeated every team in the league at least once, but, surprisingly, finished only fourth.

MOST LOSSES, SEASON

134	Cleveland Spiders (N.L.), 1899
120	New York Mets (N.L.), 1962
117	Philadelphia Athletics (A.L.), 1916
115	Boston Braves (N.L.), 1935
113	Pittsburgh Innocents (N.L.), 1890
113	Washington Senators (A.L.), 1904
112	Pittsburgh Pirates (N.L.), 1952
112	New York Mets (N.L.), 1965

In the minor leagues, the Portland Browns of the Pacific Coast League lost 136 games in 1904. The Oakland Oaks also lost 136 games in the Pacific Coast League in 1916.

MOST LOSSES, CONSECUTIVE

The Muskogee Mets of the Class C Southwestern League lost a record 38 consecutive games in 1923. In the Holland League, the Tex Town Tigers dropped 36 consecutive games during the 1981 season.

The 1889 Louisville Colonels set a major league record when they lost 26 straight games in the American Association. They

TEAM TOTALS

finished in last place, losing 111 games, but came back the next year to win the pennant.

HIGHEST PERCENTAGE, GAMES WON

The highest winning percentage by a major league team is .832 by the St. Louis Maroons, the Union Association champions in 1884. Their record was 94-19.

Since 1900, the highest percentage has been .763 by the Chicago Cubs of 1906, as they won the National League pennant with a 116-36 record. They finished the season by winning fifty of their last 57 games.

Only eight major league teams have compiled winning percentages of over .700 since 1900.

LOWEST PERCENTAGE, GAMES WON

Granite Falls of the Class D Western Carolina League recorded the lowest percentage, .127 in 1951, when they finished the season at 14-96.

The worst percentage for a major league team is .130 by the 1899 Cleveland Spiders, who recorded a dismal 20-134 record. They lost forty of their last 41 games and were among the four teams that were dropped the following season by the National League.

Since 1900, the worst major league record is 36-117, for a percentage of .235, by the 1916 Philadelphia Athletics. Only two years earlier, they had won their fourth pennant in five years.

HIGHEST BATTING AVERAGE, SEASON

The highest batting average ever recorded by a major league

74

team is .343 by the 1894 Philadelphia Phillies. Unfortunately, their lack of pitching kept them from finishing any higher than fourth place. They had, possibly, the greatest hitting outfield ever put together. Left-fielder Ed Delahanty batted .407; center-fielder Billy Hamilton, .404; and right-fielder Sam Thompson, .404.

Since 1900, the highest team batting average is .319 by the 1930 New York Giants. Only two starters had averages below .327, but they could only manage a third place finish.

The minor league record of .327 was established by the Tulsa Oilers, the Western League champions, in 1922. This was also duplicated the next year by the Salt Lake City Bees of the Pacific Coast League.

LOWEST BATTING AVERAGE, SEASON

The lowest batting average ever compiled by a major league team is .199 by the Kansas City Unions of the old Union Association in 1884. Five of their regulars had averages under .220.

Since 1900, the lowest average has been .212 by the 1910 Chicago White Sox. They also had five starters with averages below .220.

LOWEST BATTING AVERAGE, PENNANT WINNER

The lowest batting average for a major league pennant winner is .228 by the 1906 Chicago White Sox, known as the "Hitless Wonders". They were able to win the pennant on the strength of their pitching staff, which recorded 32 shutouts that season. They also went on to defeat the powerful Chicago Cubs in one of the greatest upsets in World Series history.

The Detroit Tigers approached this record in 1968, but finished with a .235 average.

MOST HITS, GAME

The most hits by a team in one game is 53 by Corsicana in a Texas League victory over Texarkana on June 15, 1902. Twenty-seven were for extra bases.

The major league mark is 36 by the Philadelphia Phillies in a game against Louisville on August 17, 1894. Philadelphia won the game, 29-4.

MOST HITS, INNING

Chicago collected 18 hits in the seventh inning of a National League game against Detroit on September 6, 1883 to set a major league record.

MOST HOME RUNS, SEASON

The Sacramento Solons of the Pacific Coast League hit an unprecedented total of 305 home runs in 1974. This record was attributed mainly to the short dimensions of their ballpark. They were led by Bill McNulty with 55; Gorman Thomas, 51; Sixto Lezcano, 34; Steve McCartney and Tommie Reynolds, 32.

The world champion New York Yankees of 1961 hit a major league record 240 home runs. They also added 8 more in the World Series. Roger Maris led with 61 homers, followed by Mickey Mantle with 54; Bill Skowron, 28; Yogi Berra, 22; Johnny Blanchard and Elston Howard, 21.

MOST HOME RUNS, GAME

The all-time professional record for home runs in a nine-inning game is 21 by Corsicana of the Class D Texas League on June 15, 1902.

In a Class C Arizona-Mexico League game on August 19, 1958, the Douglas Copper Kings established a unique record by hitting 9 home runs, one by each player in their line-up, against Chihuahua.

The major league record for the most home runs in a game, 8, has been performed by seven different teams. It was first accomplished by the New York Yankees on June 28, 1939 in a game against Philadelphia. The last team to perform this feat was the Montreal Expos on July 30, 1978 in a 19-0 victory over Atlanta.

MOST RUNS, GAME

Back in the 1860s, scores of over 100 runs were not uncommon. During a two-year period, the Philadelphia Athletics topped the one-hundred mark eleven times.

The record for the most runs ever scored in a baseball game was accomplished by the Buffalo Niagaras on June 8, 1869, as they defeated the cross-town rival Columbias, 209-10. This included a 58-run eighth inning.

The professional league record was set by the Corsicana Oil City when they scored 51 runs on June 15, 1902 against Texarkana in a Texas League game. The final score was 51-3. The previous record of 49 had been established in 1871 by the Philadelphia Athletics in the old National Assocation.

Chicago (N.L.) scored a major league record 36 runs in a game against Louisville on June 29, 1897. They also collected thirty-two hits and were aided by nine Louisville errors. The final score was 36-7.

TEAM TOTALS

MOST RUNS, INNING

In a Class D Coastal Plain League game, the Tarboro Athletics scored 24 runs in the fifth inning against Wilson to set an all-time professional record on June 2, 1951. Twenty-five batters came to the plate before the first out was recorded. The final score was 31-4.

On July 4, 1873, the Boston Red Stockings scored 21 times in the ninth inning of a National Association victory over Philadelphia (24-19).

The most runs scored in an inning of a major league game is 18. Chicago (N.L.) exploded for this record in the seventh inning against Detroit on September 6, 1883. The record since 1900 is held by the Boston Red Sox, who scored 17 times during the 48-minute seventh inning against Detroit on June 18, 1953.

MOST STOLEN BASES, GAME

On July 23, 1907, the Austin Senators stole 23 bases in a Class C Texas League game against San Antonio en route to a 44-0 victory.

The Philadelphia Athletics stole 19 bases in a game against Syracuse on April 22, 1890 to set a major league record. Philadelphia won the game, 17-6.

MOST STOLEN BASES, INNING

In the first inning of a game against Cleveland on July 19, 1915, the Washington Senators stole a record 8 bases. Credited with the steals were Danny Moeller, 3; Clyde Milan, 2; Eddie Ainsmith, 2; and George McBride, 1.

The Philadelphia Phillies tied this mark when they stole 8 bases in the ninth inning against New York on July 7, 1919. Fred Luderus, Eddie Sicking, Hick Cady and Gavvy Cravath each stole two bases, but Philadelphia lost the game, 10-5.

TEAM TOTALS

MOST DOUBLE PLAYS, SEASON

The record for the most double plays in one season is 239 by the 1931 Seattle Indians of the Pacific Coast League (187 games). Shortstop Floyd Ellsworth, second baseman Freddie Muller and first baseman Harry Taylor performed most of them.

The most double plays in one major league season is 217 by the 1949 Philadelphia Athletics (154 games). Contributing the majority of those was the infield combination of Eddie Joost at shortstop, Pete Suder at second base and Ferris Fain at first base.

MOST DOUBLE PLAYS, GAME

The major league record of 7 double plays in one 9-inning game was set by the New York Yankees on August 14, 1942 in an 11-2 victory over Philadelphia. On May 4, 1969, the Houston Astros equaled this record as they defeated San Francisco, 3-1.

In the Mexican League, the Nuevo Laredo Owls also recorded 7 double plays against Mexico City on September 29, 1949. In a 7-inning game on August 9, 1967, Raleigh executed a double play in each inning against Burlington in the Class A Carolina League.

MOST TRIPLE PLAYS, SEASON

The record for the most triple plays in one season was set in 1959 when the Reno Silver Sox recorded 4 in the Class C California League.

The major league record is 3, held by eight different teams. The first team to accomplish this was the Cincinnati Reds of the American Association in 1882. It was last performed by the Boston Red Sox and Oakland Athletics in 1979.

79

TEAM TOTALS

In the Italian League, Lazio executed 3 triple plays in 1969, while Milan tied the record in 1973.

FIRST TRIPLE PLAY

The first recorded triple play occurred on July 22, 1860. In a game against Baltimore, left-fielder James Creighton of the Brooklyn Excelsiors is said to have made an outstanding diving catch, and then threw to the infield to catch both runners off base.

St. Louis (N.L.) recorded the first triple play in the majors on June 29, 1876. It was accomplished by shortstop Dickey Pearce, first baseman Harmon Dehlman and third baseman Joe Battin in a game against New York.

LONGEST GAME

In an International League game on April 18, 1981, the Rochester Red Wings and the Pawtucket Red Sox played 32 innings to establish an all-time record. The game was halted at 4 a.m. with the score tied at 2-2. It was continued on June 23rd, as Pawtucket scored in the bottom of the 33rd inning to win the game, 3-2.

The longest major league game ever played took place on May 1, 1920. The Boston Braves and Brooklyn, the National League champions that year, battled to a 1-1 tie for 26 innings before the game was finally called because of darkness. Joe Oeschger of Boston and Leon Cadore of Brooklyn pitched the entire game.

SHORTEST GAME

Only 32 minutes were needed to complete a Southern Association game between the Mobile Gulls and the Atlanta Crackers on September 19, 1910. The league, with the cooperation of the players, conducted this game as an experiment, attempting to play as quickly as possible. The batters swung at every good pitch and little time was taken between pitches. There were no strikeouts and only one walk. Mobile won, 2-1.

The shortest regulation nine-inning game in major league history required only 51 minutes to complete. It took place on September 28, 1919 in the first game of a doubleheader, as the New York Giants defeated Philadelphia, 6-1.

TRIPLEHEADERS

On September 1, 1890, Brooklyn, the National League champions, defeated Pittsburgh three times by scores of 10-0, 3-2 and 8-4 in the first tripleheader. The last tripleheader ever to be played in the major leagues was on October 2, 1920, when the Cincinnati Reds defeated Pittsburgh 13-4 and 7-3, followed by a Pirate victory in the third game, 6-0.

The Chattanooga Lookouts and Jacksonville Suns of the Class AA Southern League participated in the most recent tripleheader on July 23, 1984. The Lookouts won the first two games, 3-2 and 3-1, and then lost the final, 8-0. The three games were completed in 6 hours, 15 minutes.

In the old Negro leagues three, and sometimes four, games (not all against the same team) in one day were a common occurrence.

The first instance in professional baseball of four games being played in one day was on September 20, 1903, when Hudson defeated the Poughkeepsie Giants, 2-1, 6-4, 3-1 and 4-2 in the Class D Hudson River League.

TEAM TOTALS

FIRST DOUBLEHEADER

Worcester defeated Providence, 4-3, and then lost to the Grays, 8-6, in the first major league doubleheader on September 25, 1882. Prior to this, several teams had played two games in one day, but this was the first instance of games being played back-to-back.

The last-place Worcester club moved to Philadelphia the next year, where they became known as the Phillies.

FIRST BASEBALL TEAM

The first organized baseball team was the Knickerbocker Baseball and Social Club of New York, which had been formed on September 23, 1845. The members usually met two or three times a week and divided into two teams. The games lasted until one team scored 21 runs. Thirteen of these intra-club games were played that season, with the first being held on October 6.

On June 19, 1846, they participated in the first regulation baseball game between two clubs. This took place at the cricket grounds known as Elysian Fields in Hoboken, New Jersey. The New York Nine defeated the Knickerbockers, 23-1, in this historic event.

FIRST PROFESSIONAL TEAM

In 1869, the Cincinnati Red Stockings became the first professional baseball team. The "reported" salaries for their three top players were: shortstop George Wright, $1,400; captain and center-fielder Harry Wright, $1,200; and pitcher Asa Brainard, $1,100. The total team payroll was $9,500.

TEAM TOTALS

EARLY AIR TRAVEL

The Kelly Aviation Field team of San Antonio, Texas was flown to a game in Laredo on July 27, 1918. The 150-mile trip took a little over an hour.

The first professional team to travel by air was the Hollywood Stars of the Pacific Coast League. They flew from Seattle to Portland on July 15, 1928.

On July 30, 1936, the Boston Red Sox became the first major league team to travel "en masse" by plane when they flew from St. Louis to Chicago aboard an American Airlines chartered flight. Two years earlier, on June 8, 1934, the Cincinnati Reds had flown to Chicago. Three-fourths of the team flew, while the others made the trip by train.

FIRST INTERNATIONAL TOUR

In 1874, the National Association champion Boston Red Stockings, led by Al Spalding, went on an exhibition tour through Great Britain with the Philadelphia Athletics to promote the game of baseball. This was the first trip outside of the United States by a professional team.

They played fourteen exhibition games in London, Manchester, Sheffield and Dublin, with Boston winning eight. To accommodate the hosts, they also joined to form one team to play against England's best in a series of seven cricket matches. The Americans won six and tied one.

WOMEN'S TEAMS (Pre-1900)

Most of the early women's teams were formed for the purpose of staging baseball shows or exhibitions. The first women's "team" was the Dolly Vardens of Philadelphia. Organized in

1867, their uniforms consisted of red calico dresses and the games were played with a mush ball made of yarn.

In 1875, two teams, the "Blondes" and the "Brunettes", participated in a series of games throughout Illinois. Similar games were also played in Philadelphia, Newark and New York in 1883.

Another early women's team was the Young Ladies Baseball Club No. 1. They played against men's teams in 1890-1891 and once faced the New York Giants in an exhibition game.

FIRST WOMEN'S LEAGUE

The All-American Girls' Baseball League was formed in 1943 as the first women's professional league. This league employed modified dimensions, such as 72-foot basepaths, 55-foot pitching distance and a 10-inch ball (later replaced by regulation baseballs).

Each team played as many as 120 games a season following a league-wide spring training camp in Florida or Cuba. Among some of the teams in this midwestern league were the Chicago Colleens, Ft. Wayne Daisies, Grand Rapids Chicks, Kenosha Comets, Racine Belles, Springfield Sallies and South Bend Blue Sox. Many of the clubs were managed by ex-major leaguers, such as Max Carey, Jimmie Foxx, Claude Jonnard and Marty McManus.

One of the league's stars, first baseman Dottie Kamenshek of the Rockford Peaches, was offered a tryout with Ft. Lauderdale of the Class B Florida International League.

The All-American Girls' Baseball League was in operation for twelve years (1943-1954).

EARLY BLACK TEAMS

The Philadelphia Excelsiors won the first "Colored

Championship Series" in October, 1867, when they defeated the Brooklyn Uniques and the Brooklyn Monitors.

The first professional black team, the Cuban Giants, was organized in New York, in 1885. The players were paid weekly salaries according to position: pitchers and catchers, $18; infielders, $15; and outfielders, $12.

Before 1900, several black teams actually competed intact in the minor leagues. The Cuban Giants and New York Gorhams were members of the Middle States League in 1889. The Giants remained in the league for the 1890 season (playing as the York Monarchs) and switched to the Connecticut State League (representing Ansonia) in 1891. The Acme Colored Giants played (as the Celeron Giants) in the old Iron and Oil League in 1898. (Source: Only The Ball Was White, Robert W. Peterson)

THE OLD NEGRO LEAGUES

The first black professional league was the League of Colored Base Ball Clubs in 1887. It consisted of eight teams and was a recognized minor league. Unfortunately, it folded after the first week due to financial difficulties.

The Negro National League began play on May 2, 1920, as the Indianapolis ABC's defeated the Chicago Giants, 4-2, in the inaugural game. The original teams in this league were the American Giants, Chicago Giants, Columbus Buckeyes, Cuban Stars, Detroit Stars, Indianapolis ABC's, Kansas City Monarchs and St. Louis Giants. (Source: Only The Ball Was White, Robert W. Peterson)

Negro League Champions

Negro National League	Negro American League	Series
1950	Indianapolis Clowns	
	Kansas City Monarchs	

TEAM TOTALS

1949		Baltimore Elite Giants		
1948	Homestead Grays	Birmingham Black Barons	Homestead	4-1
1947	New York Cubans	Cleveland Buckeyes	New York	4-1
1946	Newark Eagles	Kansas City Monarchs	Newark	4-3
1945	Homestead Grays	Cleveland Buckeyes	Cleveland	4-0
1944	Homestead Grays	Birmingham Black Barons	Homestead	4-1
1943	Homestead Grays	Birmingham Black Barons	Homestead	4-3
1942	Homestead Grays	Kansas City Monarchs	K.C.	4-0
1941	Homestead Grays	Kansas City Monarchs	No Series	
1940	Homestead Grays	Kansas City Monarchs	No Series	
1939	Baltimore Elite Giants	Kansas City Monarchs	No Series	
1938	Homestead Grays	Memphis Red Sox	No Series	
1937	Homestead Grays	Kansas City Monarchs	No Series	
1936	Washington Elite Giants*			
	Pittsburgh Crawfords**			
1935	Pittsburgh Crawfords			
1934	Philadelphia Stars			
1933	Cole's American Giants			
1932	Cole's American Giants			
1931	St. Louis Stars			
1930	St. Louis Stars			
1929	Kansas City Monarchs	Baltimore Black Sox	No Series	
1928	St. Louis Stars*			
	Chicago American Giants**			

Eastern Colored League

1927	Chicago American Giants	Bacharach Giants	Chicago	5-3
1926	Chicago American Giants	Bacharach Giants	Chicago	5-3
1925	Kansas City Monarchs	Hilldale (Philadelphia)	Hilldale	5-1
1924	Kansas City Monarchs	Hilldale (Philadelphia)	K.C.	5-4
1923	Kansas City Monarchs	Hilldale (Philadelphia)	No Series	
1922	Chicago American Giants			
1921	Chicago American Giants			
1920	American Giants			

      * 1st half champion
    ** 2nd half champion

TEAM TOTALS

HOUSE OF DAVID TEAM

The House of David, a Jewish religious sect, was founded in 1903 at Benton Harbor, Michigan. Its leader, Benjamin Purnell, had an appreciation for baseball, and thus organized a team whose purpose was to raise money for the colony.

They toured the United States and Canada, playing against all levels of competition, including several major league and Negro league teams. The unique feature of this team was that all of the players were required to let their hair grow to considerable length. This was quite an attraction in an era when ballplayers had short hair and wore neither mustaches or beards.

Several of the players, such as Bullet Ben Benson, Sig Jakucki and Biff Wysong, went on to pitch in the major leagues. Grover Cleveland Alexander, Ossie Orwoll, Dazzy Vance and Dixie Walker all pitched for the House of David following their careers in the majors.

Though the House of David is still in operation, they fielded a baseball team for the last time in 1956.

ALL NATIONS TEAM

Another team that toured the country, playing against teams at different levels, was the All Nations team. They played between 1909-1938, and had the largest number of different nationalities ever put together on one team. Included were black, white, Japanese, Hawaiian, Indian and Latin-American players.

Several players later went on to become stars in the Negro leagues, such as pitchers John Donaldson and Jose Mendez. Donaldson once hurled three consecutive no-hitters for the All Nations.

FAMILY TEAMS

Another interesting team concept was the all-brother, or family team. A number of such teams have appeared over the years, though few were able to play at a highly proficient level.

The Haas Brothers team, composed of nine brothers from Naperville, Illinois, played during the early 1930s in towns throughout the state. They won most of their games and also defeated a nine-brother team from Minnesota. Bert Haas later went on to play nine seasons in the majors, while Bill, Joe and Ted played in the minor leagues.

ALASKAN BASEBALL

Baseball was first played in Alaska by the prospectors who arrived during the Fairbanks gold rush of 1902. It was in 1906, that the annual Midnight Sun Game (June 21st) was established. Each year on that day a game is played to commemorate the summer solstice, beginning at 10:30 p.m. in daylight and sometimes going past 2:00 a.m.

Semi-pro baseball in Alaska began in 1960. The Alaska League is now composed of four teams: the Alaska Goldpanners, the Anchorage Glacier Pilots, the Kenai Peninsula Oilers and the Valley Green Giants. Among those who have played in Alaska are Dave Kingman, Graig Nettles, Tom Seaver and Dave Winfield.

There have been three Alaskan-born players in the majors: catcher Tom Sullivan (1925), second baseman Steve Staggs (1977-1978) and outfielder Scott Loucks (1980-1983).

ARCTIC BASEBALL

In 1894, the "Arctic Baseball League" was organized at Herschel Island, located off the northern coast of Yukon,

Canada. This is approximately 200 miles north of the Arctic Circle.

The eight teams were composed of sailors from the whaling ships that had been frozen in for the winter. League games were played twice a week on the ice, with snowbanks built up around the field. Practice games took place almost every day. The league was in operation for two seasons, 1894 and 1895.

Ice baseball had been a popular winter game in the United States during the late 1860s and early 1870s.

AUSTRALIAN BASEBALL

Though baseball was played in Australia as early as 1857 by U.S. immigrants, it was officially introduced during Al Spalding's world baseball tour of 1888. Chicago (N.L.) played the "All-America" team, a group of major league all-stars, in a series of exhibition games in Sydney, Ballaret, Melbourne and Adelaide. In 1897, the Australian Baseball Club made its first trip to the United States to play in a series of ten exhibition games.

The Claxton Shield, the Australian baseball championship, has been won a record 15 times by South Australia.

Five-foot-seven-inch second baseman Joe Quinn played for eight different teams between 1884-1901. He is the only Australian to have played in the major leagues.

The largest crowd to witness a baseball game in Australia was an estimated 100,000 who watched a U.S. Army team defeat the Australian All-Stars, 11-5, at the Melbourne Cricket Grounds. This took place on December 1, 1956 as a demonstration game at the Olympics.

89

CANADIAN BASEBALL

Baseball was first played in Canada during the 1850s in towns located near the U.S. border.

Canada's first league, formed in 1876, was the Canadian Professional Baseball League. It was composed of six teams from Guelph, Kingston, London, Markham, Port Hope and Toronto. This league folded, though, after one season. The Guelph Maple Leafs and London Tecumsehs then joined the International Association.

Canada has been represented in the International League from 1886-1967 at various times by Hamilton, London, Montreal, Ottawa and Toronto.

The Montreal Expos joined the National League in 1969 to become the first Canadian team in the majors. The Toronto Blue Jays became members of the American League in 1977.

CARIBBEAN BASEBALL

Baseball was originally introduced in Cuba by U.S. sailors in 1866 and by Cuban students returning from the United States. The first organized game between two Cuban teams took place in December, 1874, as Havana defeated Matanzas, 51-9. By 1878, a four-team Cuban professional league had been formed. Exhibition tours by the Worcester team in 1879 and by the Philadelphia Athletics and Phillies in 1886 helped to further promote the game. It has been primarily Cubans who are credited with spreading the game throughout the Caribbean.

Winter baseball leagues are now held in the Dominican Republic, Mexico, Puerto Rico and Venezuela. They begin play in late October and run through January. The champions of each of the four leagues then meet in the Caribbean Series, a double round-robin tournament, with each team playing six games. Colombia also has a league, but does not send a representative to the Series.

The Caribbean has also been represented in the minor leagues by the Havana Cubans (1946-1953) in the Class B Florida International League, and by the Havana Sugar Kings (1954-1960) and San Juan Marlins (1961) in the International League. The short-lived Inter-American League included the following Caribbean teams in 1979: Caracus Mets, Maraciabo Oilers, Panama City Bankers, San Juan Natives and Santo Domingo Sugarmen.

Caribbean Series - Champions

1985	Dominican Republic (Licey)	1964-69	No Series
1984	Venezuela (Zulia)	1963	Panama (Chiriqui-Bocas)
1983	Puerto Rico (Arecibo)	1962	Puerto Rico (Santurce)
1982	Venezuela (Caracus)	1961	Venezuela (Valencia)
1981	No Series	1960	Cuba (Cienfuegos)
1980	Dominican Republic (Licey)	1959	Cuba (Almendares)
1979	Venezuela (Magallanes)	1958	Cuba (Marianao)
1978	Puerto Rico (Mayaguez)	1957	Cuba (Marianao)
1977	No Series	1956	Cuba (Cienfuegos)
1976	Mexico (Hermosillo)	1955	Puerto Rico (Santurce)
1975	Puerto Rico (Bayamon)	1954	Puerto Rico (Caguas)
1974	Puerto Rico (Caguas)	1953	Puerto Rico (Santurce)
1973	Dominican Republic (Licey)	1952	Cuba (Havana)
1972	Puerto Rico (Ponce)	1951	Puerto Rico (Santurce)
1971	Dominican Republic (Licey)	1950	Panama (Carta Vieja)
1970	Venezuela (Magallanes)	1949	Cuba (Almendares)

HOLLAND BASEBALL

Baseball was introduced to the Netherlands in 1908 by J.C.G. Grase, a physical education teacher, who learned the game while visiting the United States. On March 16, 1912, the Dutch Baseball Association was founded. Ten teams now comprise the major league in Holland.

Pitcher Bert Blyleven was the first Holland-born player to appear in the majors, and has played for four different teams from 1970-1984. Other Dutch players in the U.S. have been pitchers Wim Remmerswaal of the Boston Red Sox (1979-1980) and Martin Ronnenbergh of the Amarillo Gold Sox in the Class AA Texas League (1980). Hannie Urbanus, a pitcher for Amsterdam, once played in an exhibition game with the New York Giants on February 29, 1952.

ITALIAN BASEBALL

Baseball was first played in Italy in 1889 during Al Spalding's world baseball tour. Exhibition games between Chicago (N.L.) and the "All-America" team were played in Naples, Rome and Florence.

The Italian League began play in 1948 with five teams. Ten teams now comprise the major league in Italy. The championship has been won a record 11 times by Nettuno.

Among the players from the Italian League who have played in the United States are third baseman Toro Rinaldi, who played for the Tampa Tarpons in the Class A Florida State League in 1965, and pitcher Craig Minetto of the Oakland Athletics (1978-1981). Pitcher Giulio Glorioso and catcher Angelo Rizzo had tryouts with the Cleveland Indians (1953) and Washington Senators (1955), respectively.

JAPANESE BASEBALL

Baseball was first introduced in Japan in 1873 by Horace Wilson, an American immigrant, who taught at a university in Tokyo. Exhibition tours to promote the game were later made by several major league teams in 1908, 1913, 1922, 1931 and 1934. A tour by a Negro league all-star team also took place in 1934.

The annual Japanese high school baseball tournament was originated in 1929. Held at Koshien Stadium in Osaka, this

10-day tournament has become Japan's most popular sporting event.

The first professional team, the Yomiuri (Tokyo) Giants, was organized on December 26, 1934. The Japanese Professional Baseball League began play in 1936. In 1950, the league was divided into two 8-team leagues. The Chunichi Dragons, Hanshin Tigers, Tayio Robins and Yomiuri Giants joined the Central League, while the Daiei Stars, Hankyu Braves, Nankai Hawks and Toei Flyers were placed in the Pacific League. Four expansion teams were then added to each league.

Japanese League Champions

	Central League	Pacific League	Series	
1984	Hiroshima Carp	Hankyu Braves	Hiroshima	4-3
1983	Yomiuri Giants	Seibu Lions	Seibu	4-3
1982	Chunichi Dragons	Seibu Lions	Seibu	4-3
1981	Yomiuri Giants	Nippon Ham Fighters	Yomiuri	4-2
1980	Hiroshima Carp	Kintetsu Buffaloes	Hiroshima	4-3
1979	Hiroshima Carp	Kintetsu Buffaloes	Hiroshima	4-3
1978	Yakult Swallows	Hankyu Braves	Yakult	4-3
1977	Yomiuri Giants	Hankyu Braves	Hankyu	4-1
1976	Yomiuri Giants	Hankyu Braves	Hankyu	4-3
1975	Hiroshima Carp	Hankyu Braves	Hankyu	4-0
1974	Chunichi Dragons	Lotte Orions	Lotte	4-2
1973	Yomiuri Giants	Mankai Hawks	Yomiuri	4-1
1972	Yomiuri Giants	Nankai Hawks	Yomiuri	4-1
1971	Yomiuri Giants	Nankai Hawks	Yomiuri	4-1
1970	Yomiuri Giants	Lotte Orions	Yomiuri	4-1
1969	Yomiuri Giants	Hankyu Braves	Yomiuri	4-2
1968	Yomiuri Giants	Hankyu Braves	Yomiuri	4-2
1967	Yomiuri Giants	Hankyu Braves	Yomiuri	4-2
1966	Yomiuri Giants	Nankai Hawks	Yomiuri	4-2
1965	Yomiuri Giants	Nankai Hawks	Yomiuri	4-1
1964	Hanshin Tigers	Nankai Hawks	Nankai	4-3
1963	Yomiuri Giants	Nishitetsu Lions	Yomiuri	4-3

TEAM TOTALS

1962	Hanshin Tigers	Toei Flyers	Toei	4-2
1961	Yomiuri Giants	Nankai Hawks	Yomiuri	4-2
1960	Taiyo Whales	Daimai Orions	Taiyo	4-0
1959	Yomiuri Giants	Nankai Hawks	Nankai	4-0
1958	Yomiuri Giants	Nishitetsu Lions	Nishitetsu	4-3
1957	Yomiuri Giants	Nishitetsu Lions	Nishitetsu	4-0
1956	Yomiuri Giants	Nishitetsu Lions	Nishitetsu	4-2
1955	Yomiuri Giants	Nankai Hawks	Yomiuri	4-3
1954	Chunichi Dragons	Nishitetsu Lions	Chunichi	4-3
1953	Yomiuri Giants	Nankai Hawks	Yomiuri	4-2
1952	Yomiuri Giants	Nankai Hawks	Yomiuri	4-2
1951	Yomiuri Giants	Nankai Hawks	Yomiuri	4-1
1950	Shochiku Robins	Mainichi Orions	Mainichi	4-2
1949	Yomiuri Giants			
1948	Mankai Hawks			
1947	Hanshin Tigers			
1946	Greatring			
1945	Play suspended			
1944	Hanshin Tigers			
1943	Yomiuri Giants			
1942	Yomiuri Giants			
1941	Yomiuri Giants			
1940	Yomiuri Giants			
1939	Yomiuri Giants			
1938	Hanshin Tigers*			
	Yomiuri Giants**			
1937	Yomiuri Giants*			
	Hanshin Tigers**			
1936	No pennant awarded			

           *   Spring champion
         **   Fall champion

AMERICANS IN JAPAN

The first of nearly 200 Americans to play in the Japanese

leagues was catcher Bucky Harris, who won the home run title and was also selected MVP in 1937. Joe Lutz became the first American manager in 1975 when he was offered the position with the Hiroshima Carp of the Central League.

The first American to win a batting title in Japan was Larry Raines of the Hankyu Braves. He led the Pacific League in 1954 with a .337 average. Raines later went on to play for the Cleveland Indians.

MEXICAN BASEBALL

Baseball was first played in Mexico by American sailors in 1877 at Guaymas. Also, an American named Johnny Tayson is credited with teaching the game to Mexican railroad workers whom he supervised in the border town of Nuevo Laredo.

In 1906, the Chicago White Sox went through Mexico on an exhibition tour. This helped to develop an interest in baseball which eventually led to the formation of the Mexican League in 1925. In 1955, the League joined the National Association of Professional Baseball Leagues (the organization that governs the minor leagues). It is now a recognized Triple-A league.

Mexico had first been represented in the minor leagues by the Nogales Internationals of the Class D Arizona-Texas League in 1931.

Winter baseball began in Mexico with the formation of the Mexican Pacific League in 1958. Since 1971, the league champion has advanced to the Caribbean Series.

TEAM TOTALS

Mexican League Champions

1984	Yucatan	1954	Nuevo Laredo
1983	Campeche	1953	Nuevo Laredo
1982	Juarez	1952	Veracruz
1981	Mexico City (Reds)	1951	Mexico City
1980	Saltillo	1950	Torreon
1979	Puebla	1949	Monterrey
1978	Aguascalientes	1948	Monterrey
1977	Nuevo Laredo	1947	Monterrey
1976	Mexico City (Reds)	1946	Tampico
1975	Tampico	1945	Tampico
1974	Mexico City (Reds)	1944	Mexico City
1973	Mexico City (Reds)	1943	Monterrey
1972	Cordoba	1942	Torreon
1971	Guadalajara	1941	Mexico City
1970	Veracruz	1940	Mexico City
1969	Reynosa	1939	Cordoba
1968	Mexico City (Reds)	1938	Veracruz
1967	Guadalajara	1937	Veracruz
1966	Mexico City (Tigers)	1936	Mexico City
1965	Mexico City (Tigers)	1935	Mexico City
1964	Mexico City (Reds)	1934	Mexico City
1963	Puebla	1933	Mexico City
1962	Monterrey	1932	Mexico City
1961	Veracruz	1931	Mexico City
1960	Mexico City (Tigers)	1930	Mexico City
1959	Poza Rica	1929	Mexico City
1958	Nuevo Laredo	1928	Mexico City
1957	Merida	1927	Mexico City
1956	Mexico City (Reds)	1926	Jalapa
1955	Mexico City (Tigers)	1925	Puebla

Chapter Six

ARBITER ACHIEVEMENTS

HALL OF FAME

Five umpires have been elected to the National Baseball Hall of Fame. From the American League: Tom Connolly (1901-1931), Billy Evans (1906-1927) and Cal Hubbard (1936-1951). From the National League: Bill Klem (1905-1941) and Jocko Conlan (1941-1965).

In recognition of the contributions made by umpires in the Japanese leagues, Takeji Nakano, Yutaka Ikeda and Nobuaki Nidegawa have been inducted into that country's hall of fame.

MOST SEASONS

Bill Klem established the major league record when he umpired for 37 seasons in the National League from 1905-1941. Considered one of the greatest umpires of all-time, he is also known for his phrase indicating the umpire's importance in a game, "It ain't nothin' till I call it".

The American League record is 31 by Tom Connolly (1901-1931). Connolly also umpired for three seasons in the National League, 1898-1900.

Most Seasons - Major League

37 Bill Klem (N.L. 1905-1941)
35 Hank O'Day (N.L. 1888-89,93,95-11,13,15-27, P.L. 1890)
35 Bob Emslie (A.A. 1890, N.L. 1891-1924)
34 Tom Connolly (N.L. 1898-1900, A.L. 1901-1931)
30 Cy Rigler (N.L. 1905-1922, 1924-1935)
30 Bill McGowan (A.L. 1925-1954)

ARBITER ACHIEVEMENTS

29 Bill Dinneen (A.L. 1909-1937)

28 Al Barlick (N.L. 1940-43, 1946-55, 1958-71)

27 Bill Summers (A.L. 1933-1959)

26 Ernie Quigley (A.L. 1906, N.L. 1913-1937)

26 Tom Gorman (N.L. 1951-1976)

MOST LEAGUES

Ollie Anderson umpired for forty years, mostly in the minor leagues (1903-1942). He set a record by working in fourteen different leagues during his career, including the Federal League in 1914.

Honest John Kelly holds the record for umpiring in 4 different major leagues; the National League (1882,84-85,88,97), the American Association (1882-1888), the Union Association (1884) and the Players' League (1890). Kelly is also one of the few men to have played, managed and umpired in the majors.

MOST GAMES, CONSECUTIVE

Babe Pinelli of the National League never missed an assignment in more than 3,400 games between 1935-1956. Bill McGowan established the American League record when he appeared in 2,541 consecutive games during his career, which lasted from 1925-1954.

MOST INNINGS, ONE DAY

The major league record for the most innings worked by an umpire in one day is 32. The crew of Ken Burkhart, Paul Pryor, Frank Secory and Ed Sudol established this record when they worked the marathon doubleheader between San Francisco and New York on May 31, 1964. The second game lasted twenty-three

98

innings, with the Giants winning, 8-6. San Francisco had also won the first game by a score of 5-3. Total playing time for both games was 9 hours, 52 minutes.

John McCarthy and Tom Kelly had set the previous record of 29 innings in 1905.

MOST WORLD SERIES

The record for the most World Series appearances by an umpire is 18, held by Bill Klem. He officiated in the 1908-09, 1911-15, 1917-18, 1920, 1922, 1924, 1926, 1929, 1931-32, 1934 and 1940 Series; a total of 108 games.

MOST ALL-STAR GAMES

American League umpire Bill Summers established a record by working 7 All-Star Games during his career: 1936, 1941, 1946, 1949, 1952, 1955 and 1959 (2nd game).

This record was later equaled by Al Barlick of the National League. He umpired the 1942, 1949, 1952, 1955, 1959 (1st game), 1966 and 1970 games. Barlick was the plate umpire in six of the seven games.

Lon Warneke is the only person to have made appearances in the All-Star Game as both a player and an umpire. He pitched for the National League team in 1933, 1934 and 1936, and umpired the 1952 game.

FIRST UMPIRE

Alick Cartwright served as umpire in the first baseball game (between two clubs), which was played on June 19, 1846 between the Knickerbockers and the New York Nine.

Cartwright is also credited with devising the first rules of baseball and forming the first amateur team; the Knickerbockers.

FIRST PROFESSIONAL UMPIRE

The first professional umpire was English-born Bill McLean, a former cricket player. Known as "King of Umpires", he was first hired by the old National Association, where the teams paid his expenses for road trips, as well as $5 per game. He later umpired in the National League (1876-80, 82-84) and American Association (1882,85,89-90). McLean also had the distinction of umpiring the first major league game on April 22, 1876.

BLACK UMPIRES

The first prominent black umpire in a professional league was Billy Donaldson, who began his career in 1923. He umpired in the Negro National League for 15 years from 1923-1937. Other Negro league umpires of note were John Craig (1935-1946) and Fred McCreary (1938-1949). (Source: Only The Ball Was White, Robert W. Peterson)

Emmett Ashford became the first black umpire in the major leagues when he worked the Cleveland-Washington game on April 11, 1966. He served as an American League umpire from 1966-1970 and also worked the 1967 All-Star Game and 1970 World Series. His career had begun in the Class C Southwest International League in 1951.

Today, there are two black umpires in the majors, Charlie Williams (1978,82-84) and Eric Gregg (1976-1984), and three in the minor leagues.

CANADIAN UMPIRES

The first Canadian-born umpire in the majors was Tom Gillean. He umpired for three years in the National League from 1879-1881. The list of other Canadians includes Sandy Reid (1882), Bob Emslie (1890-1924), Win Kellum (1905), Ernie Quigley (1906, 13-37), Paul Runge (1972-1984) and Jim McKean (1974-1984).

ELECTRIC UMPIRE

In 1950, General Electric Co. developed an electronic umpire for the Brooklyn Dodgers' spring training camp. It consisted of a metal box, containing photo-electric cells, that encased home plate. An invisible screen of light beams formed the adjustable strike zone. When the ball passed through, a light flashed. The electric ump was not designed for actual games, though, and would not operate at night.

Other electric and mechanical umpires have been invented, but none have been proven to be practical in game situations.

LARGEST UMPIRES

The tallest major league umpires are Lee Weyer of the National League (1961,63-84) and Tim McClelland of the American League (1983-1984). Both stand 6'6" and weigh approximately 250 lbs.

Eric Gregg of the National League (1976-1984) holds the distinction of being the heaviest umpire in major league history. During the 1980 season, he weighed as much as 357 lbs.

Pud Galvin, Ken Kaiser, Stan Landes, Ron Luciano and John McSherry all approached three-hundred pounds at one time or another during their careers.

ARBITER ACHIEVEMENTS

OLDEST UMPIRES

The oldest umpire in major league history was Charlie Berry, who umpired the second game of the American League Championship Series on October 4, 1970 at the age of 67 years, 351 days.

Bill Klem worked his last regular season game on September 13, 1941 at the age of 67 years, 203 days. In 1944, he umpired some spring exhibition games at 70 years of age.

SMALLEST UMPIRES

The shortest umpire in major league history was Dickey Pearce, who umpired in the National League in 1878 and 1882, following his career as shortstop for the St. Louis Reds. He stood 5'3-1/2".

Probably the lightest was English-born Tom Connolly (1898-1931), who weighed only 135 lbs. during the early years of his career. He stood 5'7".

WOMEN UMPIRES

The first woman umpire in a professional league was Bernice Gara, who worked a game between Auburn and Geneva in the Class A New York-Pennsylvania League on June 24, 1972.

Other women umpires have been Christine Wren, who umpired in the minor leagues from 1975-1977, and Pacific Coast League umpire Pam Postema, who began her career in 1978. Postema also became the first woman to work a game between two major league teams when she umpired a Cactus League contest between Milwaukee and Oakland in March, 1983.

ARBITER ACHIEVEMENTS

YOUNGEST UMPIRES

On April 14, 1906, Billy Evans became the youngest umpire in major league history. He worked the Boston-New York game at the age of 22 years, 63 days. Prior to this, he had umpired for one season in the Class C Ohio-Pennsylvania League.

In 1958, five-foot-eight-inch Bruce Froemming became the youngest (full-time) minor league umpire when he was assigned to the Nebraska State League at the age of 18. He joined the National League staff thirteen years later.

HAND SIGNALS

Umpire hand signals to signify strikes originated in 1905 when Central League umpire Cy Rigler began the practice of raising his arm whenever he called a strike. He continued to use hand signals after he joined the National League, and this practice soon became standard procedure for all major league umpires. Several years earlier, deaf player Dummy Hoy had relied on similar hand signals from his coaches.

Bill Klem of the National League later developed standardized hand signals to signify safe, out, fair and foul.

FIRST UMPIRE SCHOOL

The first umpire school opened in 1935 at Hot Springs, Arkansas. It was run by National League umpire George Barr (1931-1949). In 1939, Bill McGowan of the American League opened a school in Jackson, Mississippi, which later became the Al Somers School for Umpires. The school has since moved to Daytona Beach, Florida where it is now known as the Harry Wendelstedt Umpire School.

Other accredited schools are the Joe Brinkman Umpire School, which began as the major league's Umpire Development

Program, and the New York School of Umpiring.

Bill McKinley became the first graduate of an umpire school to make it to the major leagues when he worked an American League game between Chicago and Cleveland on August 7, 1946.

FIRST UMPIRE TO WEAR GLASSES

Eddie Rommel, who umpired in the American League from 1938-1959, was the first major league umpire to wear glasses during a game. He wore them for the first time in the New York-Washington game on April 17, 1956. Before he became an umpire, Rommel pitched thirteen seasons for the Philadelphia Athletics from 1920-1932.

1974 was the first year that the umpire schools began to accept students that wore glasses. Although no major league umpires currently wear glasses, several use contact lenses.

UMPIRE UNIFORMS

In the early days of baseball, umpires were often attired in a Prince Albert coat, silk top hat and cane. Official uniforms were not adopted, though, until 1882, when the American Association required its arbiters to wear blue flannel coats and caps. The National League followed this example the next year. The umpires in the Players' League dressed in white during the 1890 season, but this was soon found to be impractical.

Umpires were first allowed to work in shirt-sleeves in 1936 during games played in extremely hot weather.

Numbers were first worn by National League umpires Ken Burkhart (2), Tony Venzon (21) and Bill Williams (24) during the

1970 World Series. The American League did not adopt uniform numbers until 1980. This idea had been suggested as early as 1939.

Hard plastic liners were first worn inside the caps of several National League umpires in 1985.

FIRST CHEST PROTECTOR

Jack Sheridan, who umpired in the Players' League (1890), the National League (1892-93,96-97) and the American League (1901-1914), was the first umpire to employ a chest protector. He first used a 10x20-inch leather-bound hotel guest register, which he put under his coat and held in place with the tips of his fingers. Before this, he had umpired with his arms folded across his chest. Sheridan was also the first to use the crouch position behind the catcher.

Jerry Neudecker of the American League (1966-1984) is the last remaining umpire to employ one of the inflatable chest protectors. These had originally been developed by Tom Connolly, and for many years were required equipment for all umpires in the American League.

BASEBALL RUBBING MUD

The special mud with which umpires use to rub the baseballs before each game was discovered by Lena Blackburne, a coach for the Philadelphia Athletics. Taken from the Pennsauken Creek, a tributary of the Delaware River in New Jersey, it contains an ultra-fine abrasive that strips off the factory gloss of the balls.

In 1937, American League umpire Harry Geisel (1925-1942) became the first to use this mud as a means of reducing the slickness of the new balls. Prior to this, umpires had used either a squirt of tobacco or a handful of dirt. The rule requiring umpires to rub the gloss off all new balls before putting them into play had originally been instituted in the Federal League in 1915.

The mud, called "Lena Blackburne's Baseball Rubbing Mud", was adopted for use in the American League in 1938 and by the National League in 1953.

WHISK BROOM

Whisk brooms were first used by National League umpires in 1904. Before that, long-handled brooms had been used to sweep off home plate. The change was prompted when Chicago cen-ter-fielder Jack McCarthy stepped on an unattended broom and seriously injured his ankle. The American League also adopted the use of whisk brooms shortly afterwards.

PLAYERS WHO BECAME UMPIRES

Though not a common occurrence today, a number of players were able to make it back to the majors as umpires after their playing careers had ended. The first to make the transition from player to umpire was Foghorn Bradley, a pitcher for Boston (N.L.) in 1876. He became an umpire the following season and officiated in the National League for the next six years.

Among the players in the old Negro leagues to become umpires were Bill Pierce, Jap Washington, Jude Gans, James Crump, Hurley McNair, Mo Harris, Scrip Lee and Phill Cockrell.

(minimum - 5 years as umpire)

ARBITER ACHIEVEMENTS

National League

Red Bittman	Charley Moran
Foghorn Bradley	Miah Murray
Ken Burkhart	Hank O'Day
Jocko Conlan	Al Orth
Wes Curry	Babe Pinelli
Mal Eason	Phil Powers
Bob Emslie	Frank Secory
Tom Gorman	Vinnie Smith
Butch Henline	Pop Snyder
Tom Lynch	Ed Swartwood
Barry McCormick	Lon Warneke

American League

Charlie Berry
Bill Dinneen
Rip Egan
George Hildebrand
Bill Kunkel
George Moriarty
George Pipgras
Eddie Rommel

UMPIRE EXPELLED FOR FIXING GAMES

Dick Higham, who had previously played the outfield for six different teams between 1871-1880, is the only umpire in professional baseball history to be expelled for dishonesty. He was removed from his position on June 23, 1882, after it was discovered that he was advising gamblers how to bet on National League games which he was umpiring.

ARBITER ACHIEVEMENTS

MOST EJECTIONS, GAME (One Team)

The greatest recorded number of ejections made by an umpire without having to forfeit the game took place on September 27, 1951. During the eighth inning of a National League game between Brooklyn and Boston, umpire Frank Dascoli expelled 15 Dodgers from the game. The ejections came after the Dodgers protested a call at the plate in which Boston scored, what proved to be, the winning run in a 4-3 victory.

Red Jones established an American League record when he ejected 14 White Sox from the Chicago-Boston game on July 19, 1946.

Chapter Seven

MISCELLANEOUS MARKS

MOST SEASONS, LIFETIME

Ray French, a shortstop, played a record 28 seasons in the minor leagues between 1914-1941 for fourteen different teams. In the early days of baseball, first baseman Joe Start played 28 seasons from 1859-1886.

The most seasons ever played in the major leagues is 26 by catcher Deacon McGuire, who played for twelve different teams between 1884-1912. First baseman Cap Anson played 27 seasons, but five of those were in the old National Association, which is not considered to have been a major league.

MOST SEASONS, ONE CLUB

Third baseman Brooks Robinson played 23 seasons with the Baltimore Orioles from 1955-1977, a major league record that was also achieved by Carl Yastrzemski, who played 23 seasons with the Boston Red Sox (1961-1983).

In the Italian League, outfielder Enzo Masci played 22 seasons for Nettuno from 1952-1973.

MOST GAMES, LIFETIME

The most regular season games ever played in the major leagues is 3,371 by Pete Rose between 1963-1984. He is also the only one to have played in more than 500 games at each of five positions: first base, second base, third base, left field and right field.

MISCELLANEOUS MARKS

MOST GAMES, CONSECUTIVE

The all-time record for the most consecutive games played is 2,130 by first baseman Lou Gehrig of the New York Yankees. During that streak, from June 1, 1925 to April 30, 1939, he helped lead the Yankees to eight pennants and seven world championships. He also played despite a fractured thumb, cracked ribs, a wrenched back and other ailments.

Only the weakening effects of amyotrophic lateral sclerosis (known today as Lou Gehrig's disease) were able to stop him. He died two years later. Gehrig's story was retold in the 1942 movie, "Pride of the Yankees".

The minor league record is held by Perry Lipe, who played in 1,304 consecutive games between 1903-1913.

MOST VALUABLE PLAYERS

(Baseball Writers Association of America)

	American League	National League
1984	Willie Hernandez, Det.	Ryne Sandburg, Chi.
1983	Cal Ripken, Balt.	Dale Murphy, Atl.
1982	Robin Yount, Milw.	Dale Murphy, Atl.
1981	Rollie Fingers, Milw.	Mike Schmidt, Phil.
1980	George Brett, K.C.	Mike Schmidt, Phil.
1979	Don Baylor, Cal.	Keith Hernandez, St.L. Willie Stargell, Pitt.
1978	Jim Rice, Bost.	Dave Parker, Pitt.
1977	Rod Carew, Minn.	George Foster, Cinc.
1976	Thurman Munson, N.Y.	Joe Morgan, Cinc.
1975	Fred Lynn, Bost.	Joe Morgan, Cinc.
1974	Jeff Burroughs, Tex.	Steve Garvey, L.A.
1973	Reggie Jackson, Oak.	Pete Rose, Cinc.
1972	Richie Allen, Chic.	Johnny Bench, Cinc.
1971	Vida Blue, Oak.	Joe Torre, St.L.
1970	Boog Powell, Balt.	Johnny Bench, Cinc.

MISCELLANEOUS MARKS

	American League	National League
1969	Harmon Killebrew, Minn.	Willie McCovey, S.F.
1968	Denny McLain, Det.	Bob Gibson, St.L.
1967	Carl Yastrzemski, Bost.	Orlando Cepeda, St.L.
1966	Frank Robinson, Balt.	Roberto Clemente, Pitt.
1965	Zoilo Versalles, Minn.	Willie Mays, S.F.
1964	Brooks Robinson, Balt.	Ken Boyer, St.L.
1963	Elston Howard, N.Y.	Sandy Koufax, L.A.
1962	Mickey Mantle, N.Y.	Maury Wills. L.A.
1961	Roger Maris, N.Y.	Frank Robinson, Cinc.
1960	Roger Maris, N.Y.	Dick Groat, Pitt.
1959	Nellie Fox, Chic.	Ernie Banks, Chic.
1958	Jackie Jensen, Bost.	Ernie Banks, Chic.
1957	Mickey Mantle, N.Y.	Hank Aaron, Milw.
1956	Mickey Mantle, N.Y.	Don Newcombe, Brk.
1955	Yogi Berra, N.Y.	Roy Campanella, Brk.
1954	Yogi Berra, N.Y.	Willie Mays, N.Y.
1953	Al Rosen, Cleve.	Roy Campanella, Brk.
1952	Bobby Shantz, Phil.	Hank Sauer, Chic.
1951	Yogi Berra, N.Y.	Roy Campanella, Brk.
1950	Phil Rizzuto, N.Y.	Jim Konstanty, Phil.
1949	Ted Williams, Bost.	Jackie Robinson, Brk.
1948	Lou Boudreau, Cleve.	Stan Musial, St.L.
1947	Joe DiMaggio, N.Y.	Bob Elliott, Bost.
1946	Ted Williams, Bost.	Stan Musial, St.L.
1945	Hal Newhouser, Det.	Phil Cavarretta, Chic.
1944	Hal Newhouser, Det.	Marty Marion, St.L.
1943	Spud Chandler, N.Y.	Stan Musial, St.L.
1942	Joe Gordon, N.Y.	Mort Cooper, St.L.
1941	Joe DiMaggio, N.Y.	Dolph Camilli, Brk.
1940	Hank Greenberg, Det.	Frank McCormick, Cinc.
1939	Joe DiMaggio, N.Y.	Bucky Walters, Cinc.
1938	Jimmie Foxx, Bost.	Ernie Lombardi, Cinc.
1937	Charlie Gehringer, Det.	Joe Medwick, St.L.
1936	Lou Gehrig, N.Y.	Carl Hubbell, N.Y.

MISCELLANEOUS MARKS

	American League	National League
1935	Hank Greenberg, Det.	Gabby Hartnett, Chic.
1934	Mickey Cochrane, Det.	Dizzy Dean, St.L.
1933	Jimmie Foxx, Phil.	Carl Hubbell, N.Y.
1932	Jimmie Foxx, Phil.	Chuck Klein, Phil.
1931	Lefty Grove, Phil.	Frankie Frisch, St.L.

(League)

1929	No selection	Rogers Hornsby, Chic.
1928	Mickey Cochrane, Phil.	Jim Bottomley, St.L.
1927	Lou Gehrig, N.Y.	Paul Waner, Pitt.
1926	George Burns, Cleve.	Bob O'Farrell, St.L.
1925	Roger Peckinpaugh, Wash.	Rogers Hornsby, St.L.
1924	Walter Johnson, Wash.	Dazzy Vance, Brk.
1923	Babe Ruth, N.Y.	No selection
1922	George Sisler, St.L.	No selection

(Chalmers)

1914	Eddie Collins, Phil.	Johnny Evers, Bost.
1913	Walter Johnson, Wash.	Jake Daubert, Brk.
1912	Tris Speaker, Bost.	Larry Doyle, N.Y.
1911	Ty Cobb, Det.	Frank Schulte, Chic.

MOST VALUABLE PLAYERS, ALL-STAR GAME

Though the All-Star Game was first played in 1933, MVP selections were not made until 1962. From 1962-1969, the Arch Ward Memorial Award was presented to the All-Star Game MVP, selected by the official scorers. Since 1970, the Commissioner's Trophy has been awarded to the Most Valuable Player chosen by the media.

Willie Mays, Steve Garvey and Gary Carter are the only players to have been selected twice.

1984	Gary Carter, Mont.
1983	Fred Lynn, Cal.

MISCELLANEOUS MARKS

1982	Dave Concepcion, Cinc.
1981	Gary Carter, Mont.
1980	Ken Griffey, Cinc.
1979	Dave Parker, Pitt.
1978	Steve Garvey, L.A.
1977	Don Sutton, L.A.
1976	George Foster, Cinc.
1975	Bill Madlock, Chic. John Matlack, N.Y.
1974	Steve Garvey, L.A.
1973	Bobby Bonds, S.F.
1972	Joe Morgan, Cinc.
1971	Frank Robinson, Balt.
1970	Carl Yastrzemski, Bost.
1969	Willie McCovey, S.F.
1968	Willie Mays, S.F.
1967	Tony Perez, Cinc.
1966	Brooks Robinson, Balt.
1965	Juan Marichal, S.F.
1964	Johnny Callison, Phil.
1963	Willie Mays, S.F.
1962	Maury Wills, L.A. (1st game) Leon Wagner, L.A. (2nd game)

MOST VALUABLE PLAYERS, WORLD SERIES

The World Series MVP Award was first presented in 1955. It has been won twice by Sandy Koufax, Bob Gibson and Reggie Jackson. The only player on a losing team to win the award was second baseman Bobby Richardson of the New York Yankees in 1960. He had set a Series record by driving in 12 runs.

1984	Alan Trammell, Det.
1983	Rick Dempsey, Balt.
1982	Darrell Porter, St.L.

1981	Ron Cey, L.A.
	Pedro Guerrero, L.A.
	Steve Yeager, L.A.
1980	Mike Schmidt, Phil.
1979	Willie Stargell, Pitt.
1978	Bucky Dent, N.Y.
1977	Reggie Jackson, N.Y.
1976	Johnny Bench, Cinc.
1975	Pete Rose, Cinc.
1974	Rollie Fingers, Oak.
1973	Reggie Jackson, Oak.
1972	Gene Tenace, Oak.
1971	Roberto Clemente, Pitt.
1970	Brooks Robinson, Balt.
1969	Donn Clendenon, N.Y.
1968	Mickey Lolich, Det.
1967	Bob Gibson, St.L.
1966	Frank Robinson, Balt.
1965	Sandy Koufax, L.A.
1964	Bob Gibson, St.L.
1963	Sandy Koufax, L.A.
1962	Ralph Terry, N.Y.
1961	Whitey Ford, N.Y.
1960	Bobby Richardson, N.Y.
1959	Larry Sherry, L.A.
1958	Bob Turley, N.Y.
1957	Lew Burdette, Milw.
1956	Don Larsen, N.Y.
1955	Johnny Podres, Brk.

MOST VALUABLE PLAYERS, ROOKIES

In 1975, center-fielder Fred Lynn of the Boston Red Sox became the only rookie in major league history to win the MVP Award. He batted .331 while leading Boston to the pennant that year.

MISCELLANEOUS MARKS

Pitcher Larry Sherry of the Los Angeles Dodgers was the only rookie to win the World Series MVP Award. He recorded two wins and two saves for the Dodgers, as they defeated Chicago in the 1959 Series.

FIRST ALL-STAR TEAM

The first all-star team was selected in 1868 by Henry Chadwick of the New York Clipper newspaper. The following players were awarded the Clipper Gold Medal for individual excellence at their positions:

Pitcher	- Dick McBride, Philadelphia Athletics
Catcher	- John Radcliff, Philadelphia Athletics
1st Base	- Wes Fisler, Philadelphia Athletics
2nd Base	- Al Reach, Philadelphia Athletics
3rd Base	- Fred Waterman, Cincinnati Red Stockings
Shortstop	- George Wright, Morrisania Unions
Left Field	- John Hatfield, Cincinnati Red Stockings
Center Field	- Count Sensenderfer, Philadelphia Athletics
Right Field	- Johnson, Cincinnati Red Stockings

COLLEGE BASEBALL

The first intercollegiate baseball game was played on July 1, 1859 at Pittsfield, Massachusetts. Amherst College won the game, defeating Williams College by a lopsided 73-32 score. Several years later, Amherst built the first baseball field on a college campus. It was christened Blake Field.

The first international competition took place in September, 1909 when the University of Wisconsin traveled to Japan to participate in a series of eight games against the university teams in Tokyo.

MISCELLANEOUS MARKS

In 1947, the University of California defeated Yale in the championship game of the first College World Series, 8-7.

College World Series Champions

Year	Champion	Year	Champion
1984	Cal. State-Fullerton	1965	Arizona State
1983	Texas	1964	Minnesota
1982	Miami	1963	Southern California
1981	Arizona State	1962	Michigan
1980	Arizona	1961	Southern California
1979	Cal. State-Fullerton	1960	Minnesota
1978	Southern California	1959	Oklahoma State
1977	Arizona State	1958	Southern California
1976	Arizona	1957	California
1975	Texas	1956	Minnesota
1974	Southern California	1955	Wake Forest
1973	Southern California	1954	Missouri
1972	Southern California	1953	Michigan
1971	Southern California	1952	Holy Cross
1970	Southern California	1951	Oklahoma
1969	Arizona State	1950	Texas
1968	Southern California	1949	Texas
1967	Arizona State	1948	Southern California
1966	Ohio State	1947	California

FIRST INDOOR GAME

The first indoor game took place on November 24, 1887 in Chicago at the Farragut Club, an athletic club for young men. The game was played by the members, who divided into two teams. It was from this, that the game of softball later developed. The next year, an indoor game was played inside the main building at the State Fairgrounds in Philadelphia. Several major league players took part in this exhibition.

The first major league game to be played indoors was an exhibition contest on April 9, 1965 in the Harris County Sports

116

Stadium, known as the Houston Astrodome. Houston defeated the New York Yankees, 2-1, in twelve innings.

Three days later, on April 12th, Philadelphia defeated Houston, 2-0, at the Astrodome in the first official indoor game.

NIGHT BASEBALL

The first recorded instance of a game being played at night took place on September 2, 1880 in a contest between two amateur teams from Boston at Nantasket Beach, near Hull, Massachusetts. Arc lights were strung along the perimeter of the field providing dim, but sufficient, light for the game, which ended in a 16-16 tie.

A major league exhibition game was played at night on March 21, 1931 in Houston, as the Chicago White Sox defeated the New York Giants, 11-6. The first official night game in the majors took place four years later on May 24, 1935 in Cincinnati. The Reds defeated Philadelphia, 2-1.

On October 14, 1971, Pittsburgh defeated Baltimore, 4-0, in the first World Series game to be played entirely under the lights. (The last few innings of the fifth World Series game between New York and Brooklyn on October 9, 1949 had been played with the aid of the lights).

In 1979, the Texas Rangers established a nocturnal record by playing 83% of their games at night.

FIRST RADIO BROADCAST

Harold Arlin described the action for station KDKA, as the Pirates defeated Philadelphia, 8-5, in the first radio broadcast of a major league game. This event took place on August 5, 1921 at Pittsburgh. It was actually a re-creation, though, with the game being phoned in to the studio by a reporter. The announcer then repeated the play-by-play account over the air.

The next year, Grantland Rice announced the first game of the 1922 World Series for station WJZ direct from the Polo Grounds.

FIRST TELEVISED GAME

On May 17, 1939, Princeton defeated Columbia University, 2-1 in ten innings, in the first televised game. Bill Stern was the announcer for station W2XBS, which later became NBC-TV.

Later that season, on August 26, 1939, NBC televised the doubleheader in Brooklyn, with the Dodgers losing to Cincinnati, 5-2, in the first game and winning the second, 6-1. Red Barber described the action.

The first game televised in color took place on August 11, 1951, as Brooklyn defeated Boston in the first game of a doubleheader, 8-1. CBS carried the game.

Another historic first occurred on July 23, 1962, when the top half of the third inning of a game between Chicago and Philadelphia was transmitted to Europe via the Telstar satellite. This was the first live intercontinental telecast of baseball competition.

SPRING TRAINING

The first team to travel south for pre-season training was the Chicago White Stockings. Manager Tom Foley took his team to New Orleans in February, 1870 to prepare them for the upcoming season.

At the request of owner Arthur Soden, the Boston Beaneaters, the National League champions, traveled to New

Orleans prior to the 1884 season. They were the first major league team to participate in pre-season exhibition games.

The first major league team to travel outside of the U.S. for spring training was the New York Yankees. On March 4, 1913, they opened a training camp on the island of Bermuda. While there, they also participated in a series of nine exhibition games against the Jersey City Skeeters (International League) at the Hamilton Cricket Field.

Today, all major league teams operate spring training camps for approximately six weeks prior to the regular season, with exhibition games in the Grapefruit League (Florida) or Cactus League (Arizona).

FIRST LEAGUE

On March 10, 1858, the first league was formed at a convention represented by three delegates from each of the 25 clubs. The name chosen was the National Association of Base Ball Players. New York defeated Brooklyn, 22-18, in the first game, which took place on July 20, 1858 at the Fashion Race Course in New York. This loosely organized league remained in operation through the 1870 season.

FIRST MINOR LEAGUE

The International Association was formed in 1877 as the first minor league. The teams included were the Columbus Buckeyes, Guelph Maple Leafs, London Tecumsehs, Lynn Live Oaks, Manchester (N.H.), Pittsburgh Alleghenies and the Rochester Hop Bitters.

London won the championship, finishing one game ahead of Pittsburgh. The league folded after the 1878 season.

LITTLE LEAGUE

The Little League, founded in 1939 by Carl Stotz as a 3-team league in Williamsport, Pennsylvania, has become the starting point for many major league players. Over 300 Little League graduates now play in the majors. The list includes George Brett, Steve Carlton, Steve Garvey, Nolan Ryan and Mike Schmidt.

Eight years after its inception, the Little League held its first World Series. In the championship game that year, Williamsport defeated Lock Haven, 16-7. The first foreign representative in the Little League World Series was a team from Montreal in 1952. Japan was first represented in 1962 by Kunitachi. Today, there are over 9,000 leagues in thirty-one countries.

Little League World Series - Champions

1984	Seoul, South Korea	1965	Windsor Locks, Connecticut
1983	Marietta, Georgia	1964	Staten Island, New York
1982	Kirkland, Washington	1963	Granada Hills, California
1981	Taichung, Taiwan	1962	San Jose, California
1980	Hualien, Taiwan	1961	El Cajon, California
1979	Pu-tzu, Taiwan	1960	Levittown, Pennsylvania
1978	Pingtung, Taiwan	1959	Hamtramck, Michigan
1977	Li-Teh, Taiwan	1958	Monterrey, Mexico
1976	Tokyo, Japan	1957	Monterrey, Mexico
1975	Lakewood, New Jersey	1956	Roswell, New Mexico
1974	Kaohsiung, Taiwan	1955	Morrisville, Pennsylvania
1973	Tainan, Taiwan	1954	Schenectady, New York
1972	Taipei, Taiwan	1953	Birmingham, Alabama
1971	Tainan, Taiwan	1952	Norwalk, Connecticut
1970	Wayne, New Jersey	1951	Stamford, Connecticut
1969	Taipei, Taiwan	1950	Houston, Texas
1968	Wakayama, Japan	1949	Hammonton, New Jersey
1967	Tokyo, Japan	1948	Lock Haven, Pennsylvania
1966	Houston, Texas	1947	Williamsport, Pennsylvania

MISCELLANEOUS MARKS

SIX-MAN BASEBALL

In 1939, Stephen Epler invented a modified version of the game, called "six-man baseball". Each team is composed of six players: a pitcher, catcher, two infielders and two outfielders. Instead of playing on a 4-base diamond, the infield is triangular with 3 bases.

Also, two strikes on the batter constitute a strikeout and three balls for a walk. A game consists of six innings. The game of six-man baseball was first demonstrated on August 9, 1939 at Columbia University.

WELSH BASEBALL

Another version of the game is known as Welsh baseball, which today is played mainly in South Wales and northwest England. The game is played on a diamond-shaped infield with 11 players per team. Each base is represented by a pole stuck in the ground which must be touched by the baserunners. The bat and ball more closely resemble those used in cricket. Gloves and other protective equipment are not allowed and pitches are delivered underhand. All 11 members of a team bat before the inning is completed.

International games between Welsh and English teams have been played since 1908. The first game to be televised was in 1971 by the B.B.C. Today, the Welsh National Baseball League consists of approximately 60 teams in eight divisions.

LARGEST FIELD

The largest enclosed playing field in a major league stadium was that of Braves Field in Boston. The distance down both foul lines was 402 feet and 550 feet to the center field fence.

MISCELLANEOUS MARKS

Built in 1915, owner Jim Gaffney wanted the playing field to be so large that it would be possible to hit a home run inside the park in any direction. This is exactly what happened, as over 200 inside-the-park home runs were hit there during the next twelve seasons.

In 1928, to increase seating capacity, the left field fence was moved in to 353 feet and the center field fence to 387 feet.

Braves Field also featured one of baseball's first electronic scoreboards in 1949. It was last used as a major league stadium in 1952, as the Braves moved to Milwaukee the next year.

BALLPARK INNOVATIONS

The first enclosed baseball field was the Union Grounds in Brooklyn. It opened May 15, 1862 and served as the home field for the Morrisania Unions.

In 1895, the Cincinnati Reds became the first major league club to paint their center field fence black in order to provide the batters with a dark background against which to hit.

The first stadium to have the distances from home plate painted on the fences was Yankee Stadium in New York, which opened on April 18, 1923.

In 1948, Ebbetts Field in Brooklyn became the first stadium to have its outfield walls padded with foam rubber. This was an attempt by owner Branch Rickey to minimize the injuries to left-fielder Pete Reiser, who had crashed into the wall on several occasions.

Another safety feature, the warning track along the outfield fences, became a part of major league playing fields in 1950. Prior to this, some parks had slight inclines built up against the fence.

MISCELLANEOUS MARKS

ATTENDANCE RECORDS, SEASON

The attendance record for one season is held by the Los Angeles Dodgers. In 1982, they drew 3,608,881 fans to Dodger Stadium during their 81 home games, which was 80 percent of their stadium capacity. (The record for ratio of admissions compared to capacity is 89 percent by the Boston Red Sox in 1979.) The Dodgers are also the only team to ever exceed the three-million mark.

Previous attendance milestones were accomplished by the New York Yankees with 1,289,422 in 1920 and 2,265,512 in 1946.

In 1984, the Yomiuri (Tokyo) Giants of the Japanese Central League drew a total of 2,974,000 fans. They played 65 games at Korakuen Stadium that season.

The minor league record of 1,052,438 was set by the Louisville Redbirds of the American Association in 1983.

ATTENDANCE RECORDS, GAME

The all-time attendance record was set on August 12, 1936 at the Olympic Stadium in Berlin, Germany. An estimated 110,000 spectators saw the "World Champions" team defeat the "Olympics" team, 6-5, in a demonstration game at the 1936 Olympics.

The largest attendance for a game between two major league teams is 93,103, set on May 7, 1959 when the New York Yankees defeated the Dodgers, 6-2, in an exhibition game at the Los Angeles Coliseum.

The minor league record of 65,666 was set on July 3, 1982 in an American Association game at Mile High Stadium in Denver. The Omaha Royals defeated the Denver Bears in that game, 7-4.

The smallest attendance for a major league game is 12. In a rainstorm, Chicago defeated the Trojans, 10-8, in the last game of the season at Troy, New York on September 27, 1881.

MISCELLANEOUS MARKS

STADIUM LONGEVITY RECORDS

Sportsman's Park in St. Louis was used as a major league field from 1876-1966 (not consecutively, though, as the stadium was unoccupied from 1878-1881 and 1892-1901). The 77 years that it was in use is a record for a major league stadium. From 1920-1953, it was used by both the Browns and Cardinals. In 1953, it was renamed Busch Stadium.

The all-time longevity record is held by the Sulpher Dell in Nashville, which was opened in 1866. The Nashville Volunteers of the Southern Association played there for the last time in 1963.

SEVENTH-INNING STRETCH

According to legend, the seventh-inning stretch is believed to have first taken place in June, 1882 during an exhibition game between Manhattan College and the New York Metropolitans. Brother Jasper, Manhattan's coach, saw that the student fans were getting restless. When Manhattan came to bat in the seventh inning, he encouraged the students to rise and stretch for a few minutes.

This soon became a regular practice at all Manhattan games. It was during one of their annual exhibition games against the New York Giants, that the stretch was copied by the professional league fans.

On October 18, 1889, the fans at New York took a stretch during the seventh inning of the opening game in the World Series between the Giants and Brooklyn.

FIRST BASEBALL UNIFORM

The Knickerbocker Club of New York (organized in 1845) voted to adopt the first uniforms at a team meeting on April 24,

1849. The selected uniform consisted of a white flannel shirt, long navy blue pants and a straw hat.

In 1855, mohair hats replaced the straw ones and a leather belt was added to the uniform. Except for slight changes in the hat, this uniform style was used by the Knickerbockers for the next 30 years.

FIRST UNIFORM NUMBERS

Numbers on uniforms were first advocated in 1894 by Chicago (N.L.) owner Jim Hart. It wasn't until twenty-two years later, that Jack Graney of the Cleveland Indians became the first player to appear in a game with a number on his uniform. On June 26, 1916, he led off the first inning of a game in which all of the Cleveland players had numbers sewn on their sleeves. For some reason, though, the players thought that this was degrading, and the numbers were later removed.

Thirteen years later, on April 16, 1929, the Indians became the first team to wear numbers on the backs of their home uniforms. That same season, the New York Yankees wore numbers on the backs of both their home and away uniforms.

This became an accepted practice by American League teams in 1931 and National League in 1933.

The Chicago White Sox, in 1960, became the first major league team to have players' names appear on the uniform as an aid to player identification.

UNIQUE NUMBERS

Outfielder Carlos May of the Chicago White Sox was the only player in the major leagues to ever wear his birthdate on his uniform. The number on the back of his jersey, under his name, was 17. He was born on May 17, 1948.

MISCELLANEOUS MARKS

Pitcher Bill Voiselle wore the name of his hometown on the back of his uniform when he played for the Boston Braves and Chicago Cubs (1947-1950). He was from Ninety Six, South Carolina.

The highest number to have been worn by a major league player is 99, which outfielder Willie Crawford of Oakland wore in 1977. (During spring training, several non-roster players have worn No. 100.) The lowest uniform number is 0, first worn by outfielder Al Oliver of the Texas Rangers in 1978. Eddie Gaedel had No. 1/8 on the back of his uniform on August 19, 1951.

The first player to have his number retired was Lou Gehrig. The New York Yankees retired his No. 4 in 1939.

FIRST PLAYERS TO WEAR GLASSES

Will White, who pitched for four different teams between 1877-1886, was the first major league player to wear glasses during a game. It was thought at the time, that to wear glasses on the field was not only a serious handicap, but extremely dangerous as well.

It wasn't until April 19, 1915, when Lee Meadows, a pitcher for the St. Louis Cardinals, became the next player to wear glasses. He was followed shortly afterwards by another pitcher, Carmen Hill. They both became 20-game winners and, in 1927, led Pittsburgh to the pennant.

The first non-pitcher to wear glasses in the major leagues was Specs Toporcer, a shortstop for the Cardinals in 1921. In 1951, Clint Courtney of the New York Yankees became the first major league catcher to wear them.

MISCELLANEOUS MARKS

Left-fielder Fred Clarke of the Pittsburgh Pirates (1894-1915) was the first player to wear smoked glasses (sunglasses) in order to shade his eyes from the sun's glare.

MUSTACHES & BEARDS

Mustaches were very popular among players in the late 1800s. But at the turn of the century, they went out of style and, except for several players, disappeared from the major leagues.

First baseman Jake Beckley, who finished his major league career in St. Louis (1904-1907), wore a mustache which had a bit of handlebar, as did that of Philadelphia shortstop Monte Cross, who played until 1907. John Titus, who played right field for Philadelphia and Boston from 1903-1913, sported a stubby mustache.

Catcher Wally Schang of the Philadelphia Athletics had a mustache as late as 1914, and was the last player to wear one in a regular season game until April 15, 1972, when right-fielder Reggie Jackson of the Oakland Athletics first wore one on opening day.

House of David pitcher Allen Benson, who played briefly for the Washington Senators in 1934, was the first player to wear a beard since Jack Remsen in 1884.

The only major league manager to have worn a full-length beard was Gus Schmelz (1884-1897).

COLORED BASEBALLS

During the 1870s, the standard ball for professional and college games was red. It was believed that the fielders would have an easier time spotting a red ball in the sunny skies, rather than a white one. But in the latter part of the '70s, the white ball came back into use. The red ball disappeared after 1880, never to be used again.

On August 28, 1928, in an American Association doubleheader between Milwaukee and Louisville, yellow balls were used as an experiment to determine if their visibility was greater and discoloration less than white balls.

The Brooklyn Dodgers, at the suggestion of general manager Larry MacPhail, used a yellow ball (regulation National League balls that were dyed yellow) in a game against St. Louis on August 2, 1938. The Dodgers won, 6-2. The following year, the Dodgers also used yellow balls in three games; twice against St. Louis and once against Chicago.

When the Houston Astrodome was first opened in 1965, experiments with red, yellow and orange balls were made to test the indoor visibility.

At the request of owner Charlie Finley, Oakland used orange baseballs in a Cactus League game against Cleveland on March 29, 1973. The Indians won the game, 11-5. These were also used in an 8-3 victory over California on April 2, 1973. The only time that the orange balls were used during the regular season, though, was for infield practice between innings.

BASEBALL BATS

The baseball rule book states that, "the bat shall be a smooth, rounded stick, not more than two and three-fourths inches in diameter at the thickest part and not more than 42 inches in length".

The heaviest bat ever used in the major leagues is reported to have been Hack Miller's huge 65 oz. model. One of the strongest men to ever play baseball, he normally used a 47 oz. bat during his career (1916,18,22-25). Bats of this size will probably never be seen again in the majors, as it has since been proven that a ball can be hit further by swinging a light bat fast, than by swinging a heavier bat a bit more slowly.

Except for Eddie Gaedel's 17-inch bat, the 30-1/2 inch, 29 oz. model used by Willie Keeler (1892-1910) is the smallest on record for a major league player.

The idea of metal bats was first introduced in 1944, when magnesium models were produced in the laboratories of Washington State College, School of Mines. Aluminum bats were first manufactured in the late 1960s and were approved for use on the college level in 1972. They have yet to be used in the professional leagues.

The first Louisville Slugger was reportedly made in 1884 for third baseman Pete Browning of the Louisville Eclipse. Ten years later, the Hillerich & Bradsby Company began branding the name Louisville Slugger on their bats. In 1905, Honus Wagner of the Pittsburgh Pirates became the first to have his signature printed on one.

Most bats today are made of ash, instead of hickory, with the most popular size in the majors being 35 inches. Today's major league players each use approximately 70 bats per season.

BASEBALL CARDS

The first baseball card was an 1868 team card of the Brooklyn Atlantics, which was issued by the Peck & Snyder sporting goods firm. The Old Judge cards, distributed by the Goodwin & Co. of New York from 1886-1890, was the first set to be issued. These cards were developed as an advertising gimmick for the tobacco company. One card came in each package of four cigarettes, which sold for a dime.

MISCELLANEOUS MARKS

For collectors, the most valuable baseball card is the 1909 Sweet Caporal cigarette card of Honus Wagner. According to legend, when Wagner, a non-smoker, learned that his picture was being used to promote cigarettes, he threatened the company with a law suit. The printing of his card was then halted. Only about 20 are known to be in existence. One recently sold for $23,000.

CANDY BARS

The Baby Ruth Bar is believed to have been the first candy bar to be named for a ballplayer. It was introduced in 1920 by the Curtiss Candy Co. and, supposedly, was named after New York Yankee outfielder Babe Ruth. According to reports, the company had originally claimed that it was named for a president's daughter (who had died 16 years earlier) to avoid paying for the use of Ruth's name. Also in the 1920s, the Ty Cobb Bar was manufactured by the Benjamin Candy Co. of Detroit.

In 1978, the Curtiss Candy Co. (now a unit of Standard Brands, Inc.) put out the Reggie Bar, named after Yankee outfielder Reggie Jackson. The short-lived Pete Rose Supercharg'r Energy Bar was distributed by Nutrisciences, Inc. in 1980.

The Ducky Wucky Candy Bar, which came out in 1932, was named after Houston Buffalo outfielder Ducky Medwick. This was the first candy bar to be named for a minor league player.

COMMEMORATIVE STAMPS

The Post Office of the United States issued a special 3¢ stamp to commemorate the "alleged" centennial of the invention of baseball. It was first placed on sale at Cooperstown, New York on June 12, 1939.

MISCELLANEOUS MARKS

On September 24, 1969, the Post Office issued a 6¢ stamp to commemorate the 100th anniversary of professional baseball. Commemorative stamps have also been issued to honor Jackie Robinson in 1982, Babe Ruth in 1983 and Roberto Clemente in 1984.

FIRST BASEBALL MOVIE

The first baseball movie was entitled "Casey at the Bat", a brief film produced by Thomas Edison in 1899.

In 1913, third baseman Frank Baker of the Philadelphia Athletics became the first major leaguer to perform in a movie with a plot, when he appeared in "The Short Stop's Double". The first major league umpire to appear in a movie was Joe Rue of the American League. In the 1948 film, "The Stratton Story", he played, naturally, the role of an umpire.

Baseball was first shown in slow motion in the 1945 movie, "Inside Baseball", an educational film that was written and directed by Lew Fonseca. In this film, eleven major league all-stars demonstrated the proper technique in various aspects of the game.

PRESIDENTIAL ATTENDANCE

Although Abraham Lincoln frequently attended ball games played in Washington, the first president to watch an inter-city game was Andrew Johnson. He was in attendance when the Philadelphia Athletics defeated the Washington Nationals in August, 1865. Benjamin Harrison was the first U.S. President to attend a major league game. He watched as the Cincinnati Reds defeated Washington, 7-4, on June 6, 1892. Since this game, fourteen presidents have attended a total of 113 major league games. (Source: Bob Davids, SABR)

131

MISCELLANEOUS MARKS

On April 14, 1910, William Taft, at the suggestion of umpire Billy Evans, became the first president to throw out the first ball of the season. The Washington Senators went on to defeat Philadelphia that day, 3-0.

Woodrow Wilson, who once played center field for Davidson College, holds the distinction of having been the first president to attend a World Series game. He saw the Boston Red Sox defeat Philadelphia, 2-1, in the second game of the 1915 Series. Presidents Coolidge, Hoover, Roosevelt, Eisenhower, Carter and Reagan also attended World Series games during their terms in office.

Harry Truman holds the record for attending the most major league games while in office, 16. Since Washington no longer has a team, it is doubtful that this will be surpassed.

BASEBALL CLOWNS

Baseball comedy was originally introduced back in the 1880s by the Cuban Giants, an early black team which incorporated comic stunts into their games. This tradition was later carried on by other black teams, such as the Tennessee Rats, Zulu Cannibals and the Miami, Cincinnati and Indianapolis Clowns.

Most of the individual clowns began to develop their routines with humorous antics on the field as players, and then followed their playing careers with comedy acts and shows, appearing in major league and minor league parks across the country.

The first to make a career of baseball comedy was Nick Altrock. He originally performed with Germany Schaefer from 1912-1914, and then with Carl Sawyer from 1915-1916. In 1920, he joined Al Schacht to form the most famous baseball comedy team. They performed their routines together for fourteen years. Schacht then continued the act on his own until retiring in 1968.

MISCELLANEOUS MARKS

Some of the other famous clowns have been Max Patkin and Jackie Price, who began their act as coaches for the Cleveland Indians in 1946. (Patkin recently completed his 39th season.) Ed Hamman and Bobo Nickerson toured with the House of David team. King Tut (Richard King), Nature Boy Williams and Birmingham Sam (Sam Brison) all performed with the Indianapolis Clowns team. The San Diego Chicken (Ted Giannoulas) began his career by performing at the San Diego Padres' home games in 1974.

BLACK PLAYERS

Bud Fowler, who played second base for New Castle, Pennsylvania in 1872, holds the distinction of being the first black player in professional baseball. He later played in ten different minor leagues and compiled a career average of .309. (Source: Minor League Baseball Stars, SABR)

On May 1, 1884, Fleet Walker, a catcher for the Toledo Blue Stockings of the American Association, became the first black player in major league history. He and his brother, Welday, an outfielder who also played for Toledo, were the only black athletes to play in the majors until Jackie Robinson made his debut with the Brooklyn Dodgers 63 years later, on April 15, 1947.

Prior to the signing of Robinson, baseball's "color line" (the unwritten law that barred blacks from the white leagues) had been disregarded on occasion. In 1916, Jimmy Claxton pitched in two games for the Oakland Oaks of the Pacific Coast League and Fred Wilson played for the Granby Red Sox in the Quebec Provincial League in 1935. Both later went on to play in the Negro leagues. (Source: William J. Weiss and Merritt Clifton, SABR)

MISCELLANEOUS MARKS

CANADIAN PLAYERS

First baseman Bill Phillips, who played for Cleveland, Brooklyn and Kansas City between 1879-1888, was the first Canadian-born player in the major leagues. Canada has sent over 120 players to the majors since Phillips. Among those are Ferguson Jenkins, Reggie Cleveland, Russ Ford, John Hiller, Tip O'Neill, Jeff Heath and George Selkirk.

The first of five natives to have played for a Canadian major league team was relief pitcher Claude Raymond of the Montreal Expos (1970-1971). Dick Fowler of the Philadelphia Athletics holds the distinction of being the only Canadian to have pitched a no-hitter in the majors (1945).

There have also been four Canadian managers in the major leagues: Bill Watkins (1884-1899), Arthur Irwin (1889-1899), Fred Lake (1908-1910) and George Gibson (1920-1934).

FIRST PROFESSIONAL PLAYER

The first "admittedly" professional player was English-born Al Reach, who was paid $25 a week by the Philadelphia Athletics in 1864. He was signed as a catcher and was, at the time, the best hitter in the game.

HAWAIIAN PLAYERS

Among the Hawaiians who have played in the major leagues are pitcher Henry Oana (1934,43,45), outfielder Mike Lum (1967-1981), pitcher Doug Capilla (1976-1981), pitcher Fred Kuhualua (1977, 1981) and pitcher Ron Darling (1983-1984).

Another Hawaiian player was Buck Lai, who was signed by the New York Giants in 1928, although he never appeared in a regular season game.

MISCELLANEOUS MARKS

Probably the best Hawaiian player, though, was outfielder Wally Yonamine. He began his career with the Salt Lake City Bees of the Class C Pioneer League in 1951 and later played for the Yomiuri (Tokyo) Giants of the Japanese Central League, where he compiled a .311 lifetime average (1951-1962). He also had been a running back for the San Francisco 49ers in 1947.

Hawaii had its first team in Organized Ball when the Sacramento club of the Pacific Coast League was shifted to Honolulu in 1961. The team became known as the Hawaii Islanders and won pennants in 1975 and 1976.

HEAVIEST PLAYERS

The greatest "listed" weight for a major league player is 275 lbs. for outfielder Frank Howard, who played for four different teams between 1958-1973.

Pitchers Jumbo Brown (1925-1941) and Garland Buckeye (1918, 25-28) were both listed at 260 lbs. during their careers. Buckeye also played as a guard in the N.F.L.

INDIAN PLAYERS

Louis Sockalexis was the first full-blooded Indian to appear in the major leagues. He played as an outfielder for Cleveland from 1897-1899, and it was because of him that the Cleveland Indians later got their name.

Jim Thorpe is the only major leaguer to have ever won a medal in Olympic competition. He won two gold medals in the 1912 Olympic Games.

Ben Tincup and Chief Bender both hold the distinction of having pitched perfect games during their minor league careers.

Among the all-Indian teams, the last was the Caughnawaga Braves of the Quebec Provincial League in 1935.

135

Some of the Indians who have played in the major leagues:

Chief Bender (1904-17,25) - Chippewa/Minnesota
Lou Bruce (1904) - Mohawk/New York
Chief Hogsett (1929-38,44) - Cherokee/Kansas
Chief Johnson (1913-15) - Winnebago/Nebraska
Bob Johnson (1933-45) - Cherokee/Oklahoma
Roy Johnson (1929-38) - Cherokee/Oklahoma
Frank Jude (1906) - Chippewa/Minnesota
Louis LeRoy (1905-06,10) - Seneca/Wisconsin
Chief Meyers (1909-17) - Cahuilla/California
Phil Ortega (1960-69) - Yaqui/Arizona
Allie Reynolds (1942-54) - Creek/Oklahoma
Charlie Roy (1906) - Chippewa/Minnesota
Louis Sockalexis (1897-99) - Penobscot/Maine
Jim Thorpe (1913-19) - Sauk-Fox/Oklahoma
Ben Tincup (1914-18,28) - Cherokee/Oklahoma
Chief Yellowhorse (1921-22) - Pawnee/Oklahoma

ITALIAN PLAYERS

There have been five Italian-born players who have appeared in the major leagues: pitcher Julio Bonetti (1937-1940), pitcher Marino Pieretti (1945-1950), pitcher Rinaldo Ardizoia (1947), first baseman Henry Biasetti (1949) and third baseman Reno Bertoia (1953-1962). In 1964, Bertoia had the distinction of being the first Italian to play in the Japanese leagues.

JAPANESE PLAYERS

The first Japanese to play for a professional team in the United States were pitcher Masanori Murakami, catcher Hiroshi Takahashi and third baseman Tatsuhiko Tanaka. They all played for the Magic Valley Cowboys of the Pioneer League in 1964.

MISCELLANEOUS MARKS

Later that year, on September 1, 1964, Murakami became the first Japanese player to appear in the major leagues. He pitched for the San Francisco Giants from 1964-1965 and recorded 100 strikeouts in 89 innings.

More recently, Yutaka Enatsu pitched in six Cactus League games for the Milwaukee Brewers in 1985, compiling a 1-1 record.

JEWISH PLAYERS

Outfielder Lip Pike was the first Jewish player in the major leagues. He played in the old National Association from 1871-1875 and in the National League from 1876-1881.

Other early Jewish players were first baseman Dan Stearns (1880-1889), outfielder Chief Roseman (1882-1890) and third baseman Billy Nash (1884-1898). Pike and Nash are also among the few men to have played, managed and umpired in the major leagues.

LATIN-AMERICAN PLAYERS

The first Latin-American to play professional baseball was Steve Bellan, who joined the Troy Haymakers of the National Association in 1871. He later returned to Cuba, where he managed the Havana team to three Cuban League pennants.

The first in the major leagues was second baseman Louis Castro of Colombia, who played for the Philadelphia Athletics in 1902. He was followed by third baseman Rafael Almeida and left-fielder Armando Marsans, both from Cuba. They first played for the Cincinnati Reds on July 4, 1911 and had both played previously for the Negro league Cuban Stars team.

A total of 36 Latin-Americans appeared in the majors prior to 1947. Martin Dihigo, Roberto Clemente and Juan Marichal represent Latin America in the Hall of Fame. Dihigo is also honored in the Mexican, Cuban and Venezuelan Halls of Fame.

MISCELLANEOUS MARKS

MEXICAN PLAYERS

Mexico was first represented in the major leagues on September 8, 1933 by center-fielder Mel Almada of the Boston Red Sox. He played for four different teams between 1933-1939 and batted .311 in 1938.

Other early Mexican players were second baseman Chile Gomez (1935-36,42) and pitcher Jesse Flores (1942-47,50).

Second baseman Bobby Avila of the Cleveland Indians became the first, and only, Mexican player to win a major league batting title when he hit .341 to lead the American League in 1954. He had also won the Mexican League title in 1947 when he batted .346 for the Puebla Parrots.

OLDEST PLAYERS

On August 27, 1980, Hub Kittle of the Springfield Redbirds became the oldest player in minor league history. He pitched one inning of an American Association game against Iowa at the age of 63 years, 190 days.

Satchel Paige became the oldest player to appear in a major league game on September 25, 1965. He pitched three scoreless innings for the Kansas City Athletics at the age of 59 years, 78 days. The next season he pitched two innings for the Peninsula Grays of the Class A Carolina League and, in 1967, pitched in several games for the Indianapolis Clowns.

The oldest non-pitcher in major league history was Minnie Minoso, who came to bat for the Chicago White Sox on October 5, 1980 at the age of 57 years, 311 days.

PLAYERS WHO BECAME CONGRESSMEN

Arthur Gorman, who played shortstop for the Washington Nationals in the 1860s, was the first player to serve in Con-

138

gress after his playing career. It was because of Gorman that the Washington team later became known as the Senators.

There have been four players who served in Congress following their major league careers. The first was John Tener, who pitched for Baltimore, Chicago and Pittsburgh between 1885-1890. He was elected to the U.S. House of Representatives (1909-1911) and was later Governor of Pennsylvania (1911-1915).

Fred Brown, an outfielder for Boston (N.L.) in 1901-1902, was Governor of New Hampshire from 1923-1924 and a U.S. Senator from 1933-1939.

Catcher Pius Schwert, who played for the New York Yankees in 1914-1915, served as a U.S. Representative from New York between 1939-1941.

Wilmer Mizell pitched for the St. Louis Cardinals, Pittsburgh Pirates and New York Mets between 1952-1962 and later served in the House of Representatives (1969-1975).

RUSSIAN PLAYERS

There have been five Russian-born players in the majors. The first was Jake Gettman, right-fielder for the Washington Senators from 1897-1899. Gettman, who once circled the bases in 14.0 seconds, had a streak of ten consecutive hits in his rookie year. He was followed by Jake Livingston of the New York Giants and Bill Cristall of Cleveland (A.L.), who both pitched briefly in 1901.

Other Russian players were Dimitri Dimitrihoff (Rube Schauer), who pitched for the New York Giants and Philadelphia Athletics from 1913-1917 and Reuben Cohen (Ewing), a shortstop for the St. Louis Cardinals in 1921.

Victor Starfin pitched for the Yomiuri Giants of the Japanese Central League from 1936-1955. He won a total of 303 games during his career.

MISCELLANEOUS MARKS

SCANDINAVIAN PLAYERS

There have been eight Scandinavian-born players who have appeared in the major leagues, none of whom played baseball until coming to the United States. The first was John Anderson, who compiled a .290 batting average in fourteen seasons. He batted .330 for the Milwaukee Brewers in 1901.

Norway:	John Anderson (1894-1908)
	Arndt Jorgens (1929-1939)
	Jimmy Wiggs (1903-1906)
Sweden:	Dutch Bold (1914)
	Eric Erickson (1914-1922)
	Axel Lindstrom (1916)
Finland:	John Michaelson (1921)
Denmark:	Olaf Henriksen (1911-1917)

SHORTEST PLAYERS

When three-foot-seven-inch Eddie Gaedel of the St. Louis Browns pinched hit in the second game of a doubleheader against Detroit on August 19, 1951, he became the smallest player in major league history. He was walked on four pitches in his only at-bat.

The shortest pitchers in the majors were Lee Viau (1888-1892) and Deacon Morrissey (1901-1902). Both were 5'4". Viau won 27 games in his rookie year.

3'7"	Eddie Gaedel (1951)
5'2"	Nin Alexander (1884)
5'3"	Harry Chappas (1978-1980)
5'3"	Yo-Yo Davalillo (1953)
5'3"	Stubby Magner (1911)
5'3"	Lou Sylvester (1884-1887)

MISCELLANEOUS MARKS

TALLEST PLAYERS

On September 17, 1939, Johnny Gee of the Pittsburgh Pirates became the tallest player in major league history when he pitched in a game against Philadelphia. He stood 6'9" and weighed 225 lbs.

Ralph Siewert had a tryout with the Detroit Tigers in 1944, but was unable to make the team. He went on to become the first 7-footer in pro basketball when he played center for St. Louis in 1946.

The tallest player to ever appear in a Japanese league game was six-foot-seven-inch Frank Howard, who played for the Taiheyo Lions in 1974. Rich Gale, a six-foot-seven-inch pitcher, was recently signed by the Hanshin Tigers of the Japanese Central League for the 1985 season.

6'9"	Johnny Gee (1939-1946)
6'8"	Gene Conley (1952-1963)
6'8"	Lee Guetterman (1984)
6'8"	Mike Naymick (1939-1944)
6'8"	J.R. Richard (1971-1980)
6'8"	Mike Smithson (1982-1984)
6'8"	Stefan Wever (1982)
6'7-1/2"	Slim McGrew (1920-1924)

WOMEN PLAYERS

Although women players are no longer permitted in professional baseball, several did participate before this ruling went into effect. The first was 22-year old Lizzie Arlington, who pitched for Reading in the old Atlantic League. On July 5, 1898, she pitched a scoreless ninth inning in a 5-0 victory over Allentown. Prior to this, she had played for the Philadelphia Reserves and the New York Athletic Club. (Source: Al Kermisch, SABR)

MISCELLANEOUS MARKS

On April 2, 1931, 17-year old Jackie Mitchell pitched for the Chattanooga Lookouts of the Southern Association in an exhibition game against the New York Yankees. She "struck out" Ruth and Gehrig in a 14-4 loss. Mitchell later pitched for the House of David team in 1933.

The first woman to play an entire game was Sonny Dunlap. On September 7, 1936, she played right field for the Fayetteville Bears in a 5-1 win over Cassville in the Class D Arkansas-Missouri League.

24-year old shortstop Eleanor Engle was signed by the Harrisburg Senators of the Class B Inter-State League in 1952, but did not appear in any games.

Toni Stone played second base for the Indianapolis Clowns of the Negro American League in 1953. She appeared in 50 games and batted a respectable .243. (Source: Only The Ball Was White, Robert W. Peterson)

More recently, Jackie Jackson had a tryout at first base with the Pittsfield Senators of the Class AA Eastern League in 1971.

Two women have played for major league teams in exhibition games. On August 14, 1922, Lizzie Murphy played first base for an American League all-star team in a game against the Boston Red Sox. The All-Stars won the game, 3-2. Babe Didrickson pitched for the Philadelphia Athletics in a spring Grapefruit League game on March 20, 1934 against Brooklyn, and two days later for the St. Louis Cardinals in a game against Boston. She also played several games for the House of David that season.

YOUNGEST PLAYERS

The youngest player to ever appear in a professional game was 12-year old batboy Joe Relford of the Fitzgerald Pioneers (Class D Georgia State League). He was inserted as a late-inning replacement in center field during a game against Statesboro on July 19, 1952.

In the Negro National League, George Giles was fourteen years old when he first played for the Kansas City Monarchs in 1927. He went on to compile a .324 average in twelve seasons as a first baseman.

On June 10, 1944, Joe Nuxhall of the Cincinnati Reds became the youngest player ever to appear in a major league game. He pitched in the ninth inning of a game against St. Louis at the age of 15 years, 316 days. The previous record was held by Willie McGill of the Cleveland Spiders in the old Players' League. He had pitched against the Buffalo Bisons on May 8, 1890 at the age of 16 years, 179 days. McGill was credited with the victory, as his team won, 14-5.

TOP TEN MANAGERS, GAMES WON

During his career as a major league manager, Connie Mack's teams won an unprecedented 3,776 games. He managed the Pittsburgh Pirates from 1894-1896 and the Philadelphia Athletics from 1901-1950. His teams also won a total of 24 World Series games.

Joe McCarthy (1926-1950) holds the highest winning percentage (.614) of all major league managers.

	Games Won	Yrs	Avg.
Connie Mack	3,776	53	71
John McGraw	2,840	33	86
Bucky Harris	2,159	29	75
Joe McCarthy	2,126	24	89
Walt Alston	2,040	23	89
Leo Durocher	2,019	24	84
Casey Stengel	1,926	25	77
Bill McKechnie	1,898	25	76
Gene Mauch	1,646	23	72
Ralph Houk	1,619	20	81

MISCELLANEOUS MARKS

FIRST BLACK MANAGERS

In 1951, Sam Bankhead became the first black manager in the minor leagues since 1898. He was signed as the player-manager for the Farnham Pirates, who finished seventh that season in the Class C Provincial League. Prior to this, he had managed the Homestead Grays of the Negro National League.

The first black manager in the major leagues was Frank Robinson, who led the Cleveland Indians to a fourth place finish in 1975. In addition, he played in 49 games that season. Robinson also managed the Santurce Crabbers in the Puerto Rican Winter League.

In 1962, the Chicago Cubs hired Buck O'Neil as the first black coach in the major leagues. He had previously been manager of the Kansas City Monarchs in the Negro American League.

FIRST LATIN-AMERICAN MANAGER

The first Latin-American manager in the major leagues was Mike Gonzalez, who filled in for St. Louis in 1938 and 1940 during the Cardinals' managerial transition periods.

In 1969, Preston Gomez became the first full-time Latin-American manager when he was hired by the San Diego Padres. Gonzalez and Gomez were both from Cuba.

OLDEST MANAGER

Connie Mack holds the distinction of having been the oldest manager in baseball history. He managed the Philadelphia Athletics for the last time on October 1, 1950 at the age of 88 years, 221 days. He also owned the ballclub. Along with Dodger manager Burt Shotten, he was the last major league manager to wear street clothes during the games.

144

MISCELLANEOUS MARKS

YOUNGEST MANAGER

Roger Peckinpaugh became the youngest manager in major league history when he took over the New York Yankees on September 16, 1914 at the age of 23 years, 223 days. He finished the season, but did not manage again until 1928.

FIRST COACH

In 1909, Arlie Latham was hired by the New York Giants as the first full-time coach. His duties were to instruct the players on the art of baserunning and serve as the third base coach. Prior to this time, substitute players were used to coach the bases. He coached for three seasons and, in 1911, the Giants stole a record 347 bases as they won the pennant.

Nick Altrock holds the record for the most seasons as a coach. He was employed as one of the Washington Senators' coaches for 46 years from 1912-1957.

Chapter Eight

TRAGEDIES, HANDICAPS & COMEBACKS

FIRST BASEBALL FATALITY

The first on-field fatality in baseball occurred on October 15, 1862. James Creighton, a pitcher for the Brooklyn Excelsiors and also baseball's first big star, suffered "an internal injury occasioned by strain" while rounding the bases in a game against the Morrisania Unions. He was carried from the field and died four days later. Several sources state that his death was the result of a ruptured bladder.

THE RAY CHAPMAN INCIDENT

On August 16, 1920, in the fifth inning of a game against New York, shortstop Ray Chapman of the Cleveland Indians was struck on the left side of the head by a pitch thrown by Carl Mays. The blow caused a depressed fracture, 3-1/2 inches in length, and lacerated the brain on both sides. He died in the hospital the next morning following surgery.

Chapman was one of the fastest players at the time, having once circled the bases in 14.0 seconds. He had also planned on retiring after the season.

This incident angered and upset so many people, that several players and fans tried, unsuccessfully, to have Mays expelled from baseball.

TRAGEDIES, HANDICAPS & COMEBACKS

OTHER ON-FIELD FATALITIES

Though there have been a number of reported deaths in baseball, relatively few have occurred in professional competition. Following are several cases:

The first fatality since 1900 resulted on August 9, 1906, when Tom Burke of Lynn was struck in the temple by a pitch delivered by Joe Yeager of Fall River. This took place in the sixth inning of a Class B New England League game. Burke died two days later.

* * *

Johnny Dodge, a third baseman for the Mobile Bears of the Southern Association died from injuries he received when struck in the face from a pitch thrown by Tom Rogers of Nashville in a game on June 18, 1916. Dodge had played for the Philadelphia Phillies and Cincinnati Reds several years earlier.

* * *

The last known fatality from a pitched ball occurred in a Class D Alabama-Florida League game. On June 2, 1951, outfielder Ottis Johnson of Dothan was struck by a fastball thrown by Jack Clifton of Headland. He died eight days later.

* * *

On April 5, 1953, Herb Gorman of the San Diego Padres suffered a heart attack while playing left field in a Pacific Coast League game against Hollywood. This occurred during the sixth inning, as he later died on the way to the hospital. Gorman had played for the St. Louis Cardinals in 1952.

* * *

Dixie Howell of the Indianapolis Indians died of a heart attack on March 18, 1960, following a spring training workout in which he had complained of chest pains. Howell had previously played six seasons in the majors as a relief pitcher.

TRAGEDIES, HANDICAPS & COMEBACKS

NEAR FATALITIES

There have been many instances in professional baseball where players have been seriously injured when struck by pitched balls. Most of the cases of fractured skulls, though, took place prior to the introduction of batting helmets, which have greatly reduced, but not eliminated, the risk of injury.

Third baseman Chick Fewster of the New York Yankees suffered a fractured skull during a spring exhibition game against Brooklyn on March 25, 1920. He was struck in the temple by a Jeff Pfeffer pitch in the first inning. The blow rendered him speechless for about one week afterwards. After the insertion of a metal plate in his head, he was able to play later that season.

* * *

On August 26, 1936, rookie right-fielder Eddie Wilson of the Brooklyn Dodgers suffered a fractured skull in a game against Pittsburgh. He was struck on the side of the head by a Mace Brown fastball in the fifth inning. His average at the time was .347, but after the injury, he played only 36 more games in the majors.

* * *

Mickey Cochrane, a catcher for the Detroit Tigers, was struck in the right temple with a pitch delivered by Bump Hadley of the Yankees on May 25, 1937. It fractured his skull, left him unconscious for ten days and ended his brilliant playing career.

* * *

In a game against Philadelphia on August 27, 1954, Cass Michaels, third baseman for the Chicago White Sox, was hit in the temple with a fastball thrown by Marion Fricano. The blow fractured his skull. Fortunately he lived, but it put an end to his career.

TRAGEDIES, HANDICAPS & COMEBACKS

On August 18, 1967, Tony Conigliaro of the Boston Red Sox was struck under the left eye by a pitch from California's Jack Hamilton. He made two comeback attempts (1969 and 1975), but never fully recovered, as deteriorating vision eventually led to his retirement.

PLAYER DEATHS DURING SEASON

There have been over twenty major league players whose careers were unexpectedly cut short when they died, or were killed, during the regular season.

Hall of Fame outfielder Ed Delahanty of the Washington Senators was killed July 2, 1903, when he fell (?) off of a railroad bridge into the waters of Horseshoe Falls, New York. His mangled body was found floating in the Niagara River several days later. The facts of this case have remained a mystery to this day.

* * *

On August 3, 1940, catcher Willard Hershberger of the Cincinnati Reds committed suicide in his hotel room by cutting his throat with a razor blade. He had been in an extreme state of depression following a doubleheader in which the Reds lost both games. Ironically, he was batting .309 at the time, and Cincinnati went on to win the World Series that year.

* * *

Harry Agganis, first baseman for the Boston Red Sox, died June 27, 1955 from a massive blood clot in the lungs. He was thought to have been recovering from the chest pains that had sidelined him six weeks earlier. His batting average that season was .313. Agganis was later inducted into the College Football Hall of Fame; one of 14 major leaguers to be so honored.

149

Joe Leonard of Washington (1920), Jake Daubert of Cincinnati (1924) and Ernie Bonham of Pittsburgh (1949) all died from appendicitis.

Mike Powers died during the 1909 season from gangrene poisoning, Tommy Gastall was killed in a 1956 plane crash and Los Angeles pitcher Dick Wantz died after surgery for a brain tumor. Minnesota first baseman Walt Bond was a victim of leukemia in 1967, California outfielder Lyman Bostock was shot to death in 1978 and catcher Thurman Munson of the New York Yankees was killed in a 1979 plane crash.

* * *

Probably the greatest single tragedy in baseball history occurred on January 12, 1948. A DC-3 airliner, carrying the entire Santiago team of the Dominican Republic Winter League, crashed in a mountainous region, killing all passengers. They had been returning from a game in Barahona, when the pilot attempted a forced landing after the plane apparently ran out of fuel.

* * *

On June 25, 1946, eight players on the Spokane team (Class B Western International League) were killed when their team bus plunged five-hundred feet down a mountainside, forty-five miles east of Seattle. They were en route to a game in Bremerton. Those who lost their lives were Mel Cole, Bob James, Bon Kinnaman, George Lyden, Fred Martinez, Bob Patterson, Vic Picetti and George Risk.

WAR CASUALTIES

Three ex-major league players lost their lives in World War I. Eddie Grant, a third baseman who played for four different teams between 1905-1915 and a captain in the Army, was killed in the Argonne Forest near Verdun, France on October 5, 1918. Bun

Troy, who pitched for the Detroit Tigers in 1912, and Alex Burr, an outfielder for the 1914 New York Yankees, were also killed in The Battle of the Argonne.

Two ex-major leaguers also lost their lives in World War II. Elmer Gedeon, an outfielder for the Washington Senators in 1939, was killed on April 15, 1944, when his plane was shot down over France. Catcher Harry O'Neill was killed in The Battle of Iwo Jima on March 6, 1945. He had been a member of the 1939 Philadelphia Athletics.

Though he was not killed in combat, Christy Mathewson could also be included in the list of war casualties. He was exposed to poison gas in Europe while serving in the U.S. Army at the close of World War I. When he returned to the United States in 1919, tuberculosis had set in. He died six years later.

* * *

Gene Bearden was a crewman on the U.S.S. Helena when it was torpedoed on August 9, 1942 by a Japanese submarine during World War II. A wound required him to have a silver plate inserted in his head. He came back, though, to pitch seven years in the major leagues and won 20 games for the world champion Cleveland Indians in 1948.

* * *

On December 7, 1944, Lou Brissie, serving in the U.S. Army in World War II, had the shinbone of his left leg shattered by enemy shells during combat in Italy. As a result, there was no solid bone in over four inches of the leg. He went through 23 operations and, with the aid of a steel brace and padded shin guard, came back to pitch seven seasons in the majors.

* * *

Cecil Travis, shortstop for the Washington Senators, had his feet badly frozen while serving in Belgium during The Battle of the Bulge in January, 1945. He had previously batted over .300 in eight of his nine seasons with the Senators. When he returned from the war, he played three more years, but was only able to hit .241, .252 and .216.

* * *

Other war victims included: Eddie Kazak, who had part of his elbow shot away. He came back to play five seasons as a third baseman for the St. Louis Cardinals (1948-1952) and also played in the 1949 All-Star Game. Pitcher Bob Savage suffered a wound in his right shoulder while fighting in Italy. He returned, though, to pitch four more seasons in the majors. Johnny Grodzicki was wounded in the right thigh during combat in Germany in April, 1945. After being fitted with a steel brace, he pitched two seasons for the St. Louis Cardinals. Jack Knott was wounded during The Battle of the Bulge in 1945, and came back to pitch several games for the Philadelphia Athletics the next year.

COMEBACKS AND ATTEMPTED COMEBACKS

Comeback attempts, particularly if an entire season is missed, are difficult and not usually successful. Following are thirteen examples of players who have made remarkable comebacks from serious injuries or illnesses to play in the majors:

On July 27, 1909, while playing for the Galesburg Boosters of the Class D Illinois-Missouri League, Grover Cleveland Alexander was struck in the temple by the shortstop's throw as he was attempting to break up a double play in a game against Pekin. He was knocked unconscious and suffered the rest of the year with double vision. Fortunately, he recovered and went on to pitch 20 seasons in the major leagues. This incident was re-enacted by Peanuts Lowrey and Ronald Reagan in the 1952 movie, "The Winning Team".

* * *

Bill Hubbell, a pitcher for the Philadelphia Phillies, was struck in the head by a line drive off the bat of Tommy

152

Griffith. This occurred on May 25, 1922 in the first inning of a game against Brooklyn. The blow fractured his skull above the right ear and for a while, it was believed to be fatal. He made a remarkable recovery, though, and went on the play four more seaons.

* * *

On November 16, 1932, shortstop Charley Gelbert of the St. Louis Cardinals accidently shot himself in the left leg, four inches above the ankle. He missed the next two seasons, but came back to play five more years in the majors, though he never regained his old form.

* * *

Catcher Bill DeLancey of the St. Louis Cardinals had his career shortened in 1935 by tuberculosis. He returned to the majors on May 7, 1940 and, amazingly, played that season with one lung. He died six years later.

* * *

During the second game of a doubleheader against Detroit on August 8, 1945, rookie pitcher Jim Wilson of the Boston Red Sox was knocked unconscious when hit by a Hank Greenberg line drive. The ball fractured his skull just above the right ear. He recovered and was able to resume pitching in the majors on a regular basis in 1951. Wilson played a total of twelve seasons and, in 1954, pitched a no-hitter against Philadelphia.

* * *

On June 15, 1949, first baseman Eddie Waitkus of the Philadelphia Phillies was shot by a deranged fan in the chest with a .22 caliber rifle. It left him in critical condition, and six operations were required to remove the bullet. He was able to come back the next year and play six more seasons in the majors.

* * *

TRAGEDIES, HANDICAPS & COMEBACKS

In an American Association game on July 7, 1953, shortstop Don Zimmer of the St. Paul Saints suffered a near fatal skull fracture when he was hit by a pitch thrown by Jack Kirk of Columbus. He was out for the remainder of the season, but, against great odds, came back to play twelve seasons in the majors and one season in Japan. He also suffered a fractured cheekbone and concussion when hit by a pitch on June 23, 1956 in a game against Cincinnati.

* * *

On May 7, 1957, pitcher Herb Score of the Cleveland Indians was struck in the right eye by a line drive off the bat of Gil McDougald. It broke three bones in his face and permanently impaired his eyesight. A 20-game winner the previous season, he came back to pitch five more seasons, but never regained his effectiveness. It has been estimated that the ball was traveling at close to 120 m.p.h. when it struck him.

* * *

Two major league players: Bruce Campbell, Cleveland right-fielder (1935), and Max Alvis, Cleveland third baseman (1964), contracted spinal meningitis. Fortunately, they both recovered and were each able to come back and play six more seasons in the majors.

* * *

Second baseman Red Schoendienst of Milwaukee (1958) and left-fielder Rico Carty of Atlanta (1968) had their careers interupted when they were stricken with tuberculosis. Both recovered, as Carty went on to win the N.L. batting title two years later, while Schoendienst played four more seasons and was manager of St. Louis when they won pennants in 1967 and 1968.

* * *

John Hiller, a relief pitcher for the Detroit Tigers, suffered a heart attack on January 11, 1971. He recovered, and one-and-a-half years later, on July 8, 1972, returned to the

154

majors. The next year, he became the first pitcher to record 38 saves in one season and was selected to the American League all-star team in 1974.

ONE-ARMED PLAYERS

Hugh Daily lost his left arm several inches below the elbow in a fireworks explosion. Nevertheless, he became a major league pitcher and played six seasons from 1882-1887. He won 23 games in 1883 for Cleveland and also matched that total the next year. On September 13, 1883, he pitched a no-hitter against Philadelphia.

* * *

Harry Connama had his left arm mangled in a shipyard explosion when he was thirteen. The injury required his arm to be amputated above the elbow. He played in several western leagues during the 1910s, and once led the Northern California League in hitting with a .406 average. As a pitcher, his best season record was 19-3, which included a no-hit game against Petaluma.

* * *

Pete Gray lost his right arm when he was a boy. At the age of six, he fell off of a grocery wagon. His arm was mangled when it was caught in one of the wheels, requiring it to be amputated above the elbow. He was selected MVP in the Southern Association in 1944, as he batted .333 and stole 68 bases. Gray made it to the major leagues in 1945 as an outfielder with the St. Louis Browns.

* * *

Steve "Nub" Anderson was hit by a truck as a child. As a result, it was necessary for his left arm to be amputated. Anderson played first base for the Indianapolis Clowns from

1966-68 and 1972-73. He also appeared in the 1976 movie, "The Bingo Long Traveling All-Stars and Motor Kings".

Among the other one-armed players who overcame this handicap to play professional baseball were: Pedro Barbosa, despite having lost his left arm in a farming accident at the age of eleven, went on to play first base for the Monterrey Sultans of the Mexican League. Chester Morrissey pitched for the Douglas Trojans of the Class D Georgia State League in 1949, despite the fact that his right arm had been amputated. He had severely injured it in a fireworks explosion when he was eight years old.

ONE-LEGGED PLAYERS

On May 21, 1944, Bert Shepard's P-38 plane was shot down over Germany during World War II. His right leg was mangled in the wreckage, requiring it to be amputated just below the knee. He was fitted with an artificial leg, and after returning to the U.S., went to spring training with the Washington Senators. He made one relief appearance on August 4, 1945 and earlier that year, on July 10, had defeated Brooklyn in an exhibition game, 4-3. Shepard later pitched and played first base for the Waterbury Timers of the Class B Colonial League in 1949.

* * *

Pitcher Monty Stratton of the Chicago White Sox accidently shot himself with a .32 caliber pistol while target shooting on November 27, 1938. His right leg had to be amputated eight inches above the knee. He attempted a comeback after being fitted with an artificial leg, and startled the baseball world in 1946 by winning 18 games for the Sherman Twins in the Class C East Texas League. He pitched for the Waco Dons of the Class B Big State League in 1947, but was unable to make it back to the majors. His story was retold in the 1948 movie, "The Stratton Story".

DEAF PLAYERS

There have been several players who have participated in the major leagues despite having hearing impairments. The first was Ed Dundon, a deaf-mute, who pitched for Columbus in the old American Association from 1883-1884.

* * *

Paul Hines, a center-fielder for the Washington Senators, was struck in the head by a pitch during a game against Kansas City in 1886. As a result, he became adventitiously deaf, but played five more seasons and compiled a .301 lifetime average.

* * *

William "Dummy" Hoy played 14 years in the majors and was one of the outstanding base-stealers of his time. He first played center field for the Washington Senators in 1888 and though he was totally deaf, he was not completely mute, as his nickname implies. He also became only the second ex-major leaguer to live to the age of 99.

* * *

Luther Taylor, a deaf-mute, pitched for the New York Giants between 1900-1908. He led New York to National League pennants in 1904 and 1905, winning a career high 27 games in 1904.

* * *

Dick Sipek fell down a flight of stairs when he was five years old. He struck his head, and the blow left him extremely hard of hearing. He overcame this handicap and went on to play right field for the Birmingham Barons of the Southern Association, batting .336 in 1943 and .319 in 1944. In 1945, he played outfield for the Cincinnati Reds.

* * *

Pitcher Grover Cleveland Alexander (1911-1930) and outfielders Pete Browning (1882-1894) and George Binks (1944-1948) were each deaf in one year.

157

TRAGEDIES, HANDICAPS & COMEBACKS

ONE-EYED PLAYERS

Hi Jasper, a pitcher for the St. Louis Cardinals, lost the sight of an eye when he was struck by a line drive. He came back to finish his career with Cleveland in 1919.

On March 24, 1952, pitcher Bob Slaybaugh of the St. Louis Cardinals suffered a ruptured left eyeball when hit by a line drive. As a result, it had to be removed. He pitched briefly in the minors until retiring in 1954.

The first one-eyed player in the majors was Bill Irwin, a pitcher for the Cincinnati Reds in 1886. Claude Jonnard, a relief pitcher in the 1920s, also had sight in only one eye.

Tom Sunkel, who pitched for several teams in the 1940s, was blinded in his left eye by cataract in 1941. Pitcher Bob Mabe (1958-1960) had been blind in his left eye since an air rifle accident when he was twelve. Jack Franklin, a pitcher for the Brooklyn Dodgers in 1944, was blind in his right eye, as was Whammy Douglas, who pitched for Pittsburgh in 1957.

Greasy Neale played eight seasons in the majors (1916-22,24) despite the fact that he was practically blind in his left eye. As the result of a beaning in 1969, catcher Tom Egan did not have full sight in his left eye.

OTHER HANDICAPPED PLAYERS

One instance where a handicap turned out to be an advantage, was with pitcher Three Finger Brown (1903-1916). Due to a feedchopper accident when he was seven, he had no index finger on his right hand and his middle finger was bent at right angles at the first joint. This caused his pitches to have a peculiar rotation which broke and sank sharper than any pitches seen at that time.

* * *

A similar situation had also occurred with pitcher Toad

Ramsey (1885-1890). In an accident while working as a bricklayer's apprentice, the tendon in the middle finger of his left hand was cut so that he could not flex it. This resulted in his being able to grip the ball in such a way, that his pitches resembled those of the later-day knuckleball.

* * *

Another three-fingered pitcher was Willie Gisentaner. Despite a mangled left hand, he was signed by the Columbus Buckeyes of the Negro National League in 1921. He went on to complete a successful fifteen-year career (1921-1935).

* * *

Catcher Jimmy Archer played twelve seasons in the majors (1904,07,09-18) and in two World Series despite the fact that he had a withered right arm. While working in a cooperage shop when he was nineteen, his arm slipped into a vat of boiling sap. The arm was saved in surgery, but it was left badly scarred and one inch shorter than the other. During his career, the same arm was once broken at the elbow. He also suffered several broken fingers on his right hand.

* * *

When he was eight years old, Whitey Kurowski fell off of a fence and landed in a pile of broken glass. The deep cuts caused the bone in his right arm to become so infected, that three inches of his forearm actually rotted away. Somehow, his arm held together, as he was able to play nine seasons (1941-1949) as the third baseman for the St. Louis Cardinals and appear in four World Series.

* * *

Marty Marion fell down a 20-foot embankment when he was twelve years old, shattering his right thigh. He spent the next seven months in a body cast, followed by one year on crutches. As a result of the injury, his right leg was one inch shorter than the left. Nevertheless, he was able to make it to the majors and play 13 seasons at shortstop for the St. Louis Cardinals and Browns (1940-1953).

* * *

Pitcher Grover Cleveland Alexander, who won 373 games in his career, had an epileptic condition which sometimes caused him to have seizures during games. Outfielder Sherry Magee (1904-1919), second baseman Tony Lazzeri (1926-1939) and shortstop Hal Lanier (1964-1973) were also epileptics.

Ty Cobb, Jackie Robinson, Catfish Hunter and also umpire Bill McGowan all had brilliant careers in the major leagues, though each suffered from diabetes. In addition, Bill Nicholson, Ron Santo and Bill Gullickson were also similarly afflicted.

* * *

Several major leaguers were able to play despite the loss of toes. Hall of Fame pitcher Red Ruffing (1924-1947) had lost four toes on his left foot in a mining accident when he was 17. Outfielder Hal Peck of the Milwaukee Brewers accidently shot off two toes on his left foot in 1942. He went on, though, to play seven years in the majors. Catfish Hunter lost a toe on his right foot in a hunting accident when he was seventeen.

Aaron, Hank, 3, 9, 14, 111
Acosta, Cy, 34
Agganis, Harry, 149
Ainsmith, Eddie, 78
Albrecht, Ed, 29
Alexander, Grover C., 24, 65
  87, 152, 157, 160
Alexander, Nin, 140
Allen, Johnny, 42
Allen, Richie, 110
Allison, Doug, 57
Almada, Mel, 138
Almeida, Rafael, 137
Alston, Walk, 143
Altrock, Nick, 132, 145
Alvis, Max, 154
Alyea, Brant, 12
Anderson, Dwain, 2
Anderson, John, 65, 140
Anderson, Steve "Nub", 155
Anson, Cap, 3, 109
Aparicio, Luis, 46
Appling, Luke, 13, 18
Archdeacon, Maurice, 63
Archer, Jimmy, 159
Ardizoia, Rinaldo, 136
Arlin, Harold, 117
Arlington, Lizzie, 141
Arnold, Lizzie, 56
Ash, Ken, 37
Ashford, Emmett, 100
Ashman, Mike, 51
Auker, Eldon, 43
Avery, Ham, 40
Avila, Bobby, 138
Ayers, Doc, 29

Babich, Johnny, 42
Baker, Dusty, 62
Baker, Frank, 131
Baker, George, 2
Baldwin, Mark, 29, 32

Bankhead, Sam, 144
Banks, Ernie, 46, 111
Barber, Red, 118
Barbosa, Pedro, 156
Barker, Len, 36
Barlick, Al, 98, 99
Barr, George, 103
Barrett, Dick, 31
Barrett, Red, 33
Bates, Johnny, 4
Battin, Joe, 80
Bauman, Joe, 9
Bay, Harry, 66
Baylor, Don, 110
Bearden, Gene, 151
Becker, Beals, 65
Beckley, Jake, 45, 127
Beckwith, John, 1, 10
Bell, Cool Papa, 61, 64, 66
Bell, Les, 7
Bellan, Steve, 137
Bench, Johnny, 110, 114
Bender, Chief, 135-136
Benson, Bullet Ben, 87, 127
Berra, Yogi, 76, 111
Berry, Charlie, 102, 107
Bertoia, Rena, 136
Bertoni, Giacomo, 32
Bevacqua, Kurt, 54
Biasetti, Henry, 136
Binks, George, 157
Bittman, Red, 107
Blackburne, Lena, 105-106
Blaeholder, George, 42
Blakesley, Jim, 7
Blanchard, Johnny, 76
Blefary, Curt, 48
Blomberg, Ron, 19
Blue, Vida, 110
Blyleven, Bert, 91
Boehler, George, 25
Bold, Dutch, 140
Bond, Walt, 150

Bonds, Bobby, 12, 18, 113
Bonetti, Julio, 136
Bonham, Ernie, 150
Boone, Ike, 1
Bordagary, Frenchy, 5
Borden, Joe, 34
Bostock, Lyman, 150
Bottomley, Jim, 15, 112
Boudreau, Lou, 52, 111
Bowa, Larry, 45
Boyer, Ken, 111
Bradley, Foghorn, 106-107
Brainard, Asa, 82
Braxton, Garland, 36
Breitenstein, Ted, 35
Bresnahan, Roger, 21, 49, 58
Brett, George, 110, 120
Brinkman, Joe, 103
Briones, Antonio, 62
Brison, Sam, 133
Brissie, Lou, 151
Brock, Lou, 3, 60, 61
Brown, Fred, 139
Brown, Jumbo, 135
Brown, Mace, 148
Brown, Three Finger, 158
Brown, Tommy, 13
Browning, Pete, 20, 129, 157
Bruce, Lou, 136
Brunet, George, 28
Buckeye, Garland, 135
Buffinton, Charlie, 24, 29
Buhl, Bob, 4
Bunning, Jim, 36
Burdette, Lew, 114
Burke, Jimmy, 50
Burke, Tom, 147
Burkett, Jesse, 32
Burkhart, Ken, 98, 104, 107
Burleson, Rick, 47
Burnett, Johnny, 5
Burr, Alex, 151
Burroughs, Jeff, 110
Burns, George, 112
Burns, Jack, 48
Burns, Tom, 5-6
Burton, Ellis, 20
Bush, Joe, 41

Cadore, Leon, 80
Cady, Hick, 78
Callison, Johnny, 113

Camilli, Dolph, 111
Campanella, Roy, 111
Campaneris, Bert, 12, 38, 51
Campbell, Bruce, 154
Capilla, Doug, 134
Carew, Rod, 110
Carey, Max, 84
Carlton, Steve, 24, 29, 120
Carlyle, Roy, 13
Carter, Gary, 112-113
Carter, Jimmy, 132
Cartwright, Alick, 99-100
Cartwright, Ed, 16
Carty, Rico, 154
Case, George, 64, 66
Cash, Norm, 47
Castro, Louis, 137
Cavarretta, Phil, 111
Cepeda, Orlando, 19, 111
Cervantes, Ed, 51
Cey, Ron, 114
Chadwick, Henry, 115
Chamberlain, Icebox, 38
Chance, Dean, 36
Chandler, Spud, 111
Chapman, Ray, 51, 146
Chappas, Harry, 140
Chase, Hal, 46
Cheney, Tom, 30
Chesbro, Jack, 24-25
Chozen, Harry, 4
Churchill, Eleanore, 57
Cicotte, Eddie, 42
Clabaugh, Moose, 9
Clancy, Bud, 47
Clarke, Fred, 127
Clarke, Nig, 10, 15
Clarkson, John, 24
Claxton, Jimmy, 133
Cleary, Joe, 28
Clemente, Roberto, 3, 111, 114, 131, 137
Clements, Jack, 55
Clendenon, Donn, 114
Cleveland, Reggie, 134
Clifton, Jack, 147
Cobb, Ty, 1, 2-3, 16, 59, 62, 65, 112, 130, 160
Cochrane, Mickey, 112, 148
Cockrell, Phil, 106
Cohen, Reuben (Ewing), 139
Cole, Mel, 150
Coleman, John, 26

Coleman, Vince, 61, 66
Collins, Eddie, 3, 112
Collins, Rip, 47
Concepcion, Dave, 113
Conigliaro, Tony, 149
Conlan, Jocko, 97, 107
Conley, Gene, 141
Connama, Harry, 155
Connolly, Tom, 97, 102, 105
Cooper, Mort, 111
Cooper, Wilbur, 21
Corcoran, Larry, 38
Corcoran, Tommy, 47
Corridon, Frank, 43
Courtney, Clint, 126
Craig, John, 100
Cravath, Gavvy, 78
Crawford, Sam, 7
Crawford, Willie, 126
Creighton, James, 80, 146
Cristall, Bill, 139
Crooks, John, 11
Cross, Jack, 8
Cross, Lave, 47
Cross, Monte, 127
Crues, Bob, 9, 14
Crump, James, 106
Cuevas, Ramiro, 36
Cullenbine, Roy, 17
Cummings, Candy, 40
Curry, Wes, 107
Curtis, Cliff, 27
Cuthbert, Ned, 63
Cutshaw, George, 46

Daily, One-Arm, 28, 29, 155
Dalkowski, Steve, 32, 34
Danforth, Dave, 42
Darling, Ron, 134
Dascoli, Frank, 108
Daubert, Jake, 112, 150
Davalillo, Yo-Yo, 140
David, Andre, 12
Davis, Curt, 21
Davis, George, 49
Davis, Harry, 64
Davis, Tommy, 19
Deal, Eddy "New", 64
Dean, Dizzy, 112
Dehlman, Harmon, 80
Delahanty, Ed, 75, 149
DeLancey, Bill, 153
Dempsey, Rick, 113

Dent, Bucky, 114
DiBenedetto, Bill, 32
Didrickson, Babe, 56-57, 142
Dihigo, Martin, 21, 137
Dillon, Pop, 45
DiMaggio, Joe, 4, 111
Dimitrihoff, Dimitri (Rube
    Schauer), 139
Dinneen, Bill, 98, 107
Dismukes, Dizzy, 43
Dixon, Rap, 4
Dodge, Johnny, 147
Donahue, Jiggs, 45
Donaldson, Billy, 100
Donaldson, John, 87
Donlin, Mike, 52
Dooin, Red, 58
Dotterer, Dutch, 54
Douglas, Whammy, 158
Doyle, Larry, 112
Driver, Walter, 14
Dropo, Walt, 5
Drysdale, Don, 27
Dudley, Clise, 11
Duffy, Hugh, 1, 16
Duggleby, Bill, 12
Dumont, Ray, 65
Dundon, Ed, 157
Dunlap, Sonny, 142
Durocher, Leo, 143

Eason, Mal, 107
Edison, Thomas, 131
Edwards, Mike, 48
Egan, Ben, 2
Egan, Rip, 107
Egan, Tom, 158
Eisenhower, Dwight, 132
Eller, Hod, 42
Elliott, Bob, 111
Ellsworth, Floyd, 79
Emery, Jim, 51
Emslie, Bob, 97, 101, 107
Enatsu, Yutaka, 29, 137
Engle, Eleanor, 142
Epler, Stephen, 121
Erickson, Eric, 140
Espino, Hector, 9
Evans, Billy, 97, 103, 132
Evans, Dwight, 17
Evers, Johnny, 112
Ewing, Buck, 54, 57

Faber, Red, 65
Fabian, Henry, 57
Face, Roy, 41
Fain, Ferris, 47, 79
Falkosky, Dave, 51
Feller, Bob, 34
Ferguson, Bob, 20
Ferrell, Wes, 21
Ferriss, Boo, 38
Fewster, Chick, 148
Fingers, Rollie, 110, 114
Finley, Charlie, 128
Fisler, Wes, 115
Flint, Silver, 57
Flores, Jesse, 138
Foley, Tom, 118
Fonseca, Lew, 131
Force, Davy, 48
Ford, Russ, 40, 134
Ford, Whitey, 40, 114
Foster, George, 110, 113
Foster, Rube, 25, 41
Foster, Willie, 25
Fowler, Bud, 58, 133
Fowler, Dick, 134
Fox, Nellie, 45, 111
Foxx, Jimmie, 16, 84, 111-112
Franklin, Jack, 158
Freehan, Bill, 45
French, Ray, 109
Frenick, Ed, 32
Fricano, Marion, 148
Frisch, Frankie, 46, 112
Froemming, Bruce, 103
Fryman, Woody, 45
Fukumoto, Yutaka, 60, 61
Fuller, Shorty, 50
Fultz, Dave, 62

Gaedel, Eddie, 126, 129, 140
Gaetti, Gary, 12
Gaffney, Jim, 122
Gale, Rich, 141
Galvin, Pud, 24, 25, 29, 36,
   101
Gans, Jude, 106
Gara, Bernice, 102
Gardella, Danny, 54
Garvey, Steve, 45, 50, 110,
   112-113, 120
Garvin, Ned, 41
Gastall, Tommy, 150
Gatewood, Bill, 40

Gault, Ray, 33
Gedeon, Elmer, 151
Gee, Johnny, 141
Gehrig, Lou, 16, 110,
   111-112, 126, 142
Gehringer, Charlie, 111
Geisel, Harry, 105
Gelbert, Charley, 153
George, Bill, 32
Gettman, Jake, 139
Giannoulas, Ted, 133
Gibson, Bob, 27, 111, 113-114
Gibson, George, 134
Gibson, Josh, 1, 8, 10
Giles, George, 143
Gillean, Tom, 101
Gisentaner, Willie, 159
Glorioso, Guilio, 21, 28, 92
Gomez, Chile, 138
Gomez, Preston, 144
Gonzalez, Mike, 144
Gorbous, Glen, 56
Gordon, Joe, 111
Gore, George, 62
Gorman, Arthur, 138-139
Gorman, Herb, 147
Gorman, Tom, 98, 107
Goslin, Goose, 65
Graney, Jack, 125
Grant, Eddie, 150
Grase, J.C.G., 91
Grate, Don, 56
Gray, Dolly, 33
Gray, Pete, 155
Greenberg, Hank, 111-112, 153
Greenwood, Bill, 55
Gregg, Eric, 100, 101
Gregg, Vean, 29
Griffey, Ken, 113
Griffith, Clark, 39
Griffith, Tommy, 152-153
Grimes, Ray, 15
Groat, Dick, 111
Grodzicki, Johnny, 152
Grove, Lefty, 24, 34, 112
Gruber, Henry, 32
Guerrero, Pedro, 114
Guetterman, Lee, 141
Guettler, Ken, 9
Gullickson, Bill, 160
Guthrie, Bill, 98

Haas, Bert, 88

INDEX

Haas, Bill, 88
Haas, Bruno, 32
Haas, Joe, 88
Haas, Ted, 88
Haddock, George, 26
Hadley, Bump, 148
Hall, George, 10, 17
Hall, Russ, 49
Hamilton, Billy, 59, 62, 75
Hamilton, Jack, 149
Hamilton, Steve, 39
Hamman, Ed, 133
Hardwick, Vivian, 57
Harper, Harry, 32
Harris, Bucky, 95
Harris, Mo, 106
Harris, Spencer, 3, 6, 59
Harris, Stanley "Bucky", 143
Harrison, Benjamin, 131
Hart, Jim, 125
Hartnett, Gabby, 53, 112
Hatfield, John, 56, 115
Hauser, Joe, 9
Heath, Jeff, 134
Hecker, Guy, 20, 21, 24, 29,
   47
Heilmann, Harry, 2, 42
Helf, Hank, 53
Henderson, Rickey, 61, 62, 66
Henline, Butch, 107
Henriksen, Olaf, 140
Herman, Babe, 17, 65
Hernandez, Keith, 110
Hernandez, Willie, 110
Hershberger, Willard, 149
Heydler, John, 18
Higgins, Pinky, 5
Higham, Dick, 107
Hildebrand, George, 43, 107
Hill, Carmen, 126
Hiller, John, 134, 154
Hines, Paul, 16, 49, 54, 157
Hinton, Professor Charles, 37
Hisle, Larry, 19
Hock, Eddie, 6
Hogriever, George, 60
Hogsett, Chief, 136
Holke, Walter, 46
Holland, Cliff, 51
Holloman, Bobo, 35
Hoover, Herbert, 132
Hornsby, Rogers, 2, 16, 112
Horton, Willie, 19

Houck, Ralph, 143
Howard, Elston, 76, 111
Howard, Frank, 135, 141
Howell, Dixie, 147
Hoy, William "Dummy", 103, 157
Hubbard, Cal, 97
Hubbell, Bill, 152
Hubbell, Carl, 26, 41, 111-112
Hughes Pete, 17
Humphries, John, 2
Hunter, Catfish, 21, 36, 160

Iburg, Ham, 25
Ikeda, Yutaka, 97
Inao, Kazuhisa, 24-25
Iott, Hooks, 30
Irwin, Arthur, 134
Irwin, Bill, 158

Jackson, Jackie, 142
Jackson, Joe, 2
Jackson, Reggie, 110, 113-114,
   127, 130
Jacobs, Don, 62
Jakucki, Sig, 87
James, Bob, 150
Jasper, Brother, 124
Jasper, Hi, 158
Jenkins, Ferguson, 134
Jensen, Jackie, 111
Jethroe, Sam, 66
Johnson, Andrew, 131
Johnson, Bob, 136
Johnson, Chief, 136
Johnson, Ottis, 147
Johnson, Roy, 136
Johnson, Walter, 23, 27, 34, 112
Johnston, Jimmy, 61
Jones, Bumpus, 35
Jones, Charley, 10, 11
Jones, Oscar, 25
Jones, Red, 108
Jones, Tom, 46
Jonnard, Claude, 84, 158
Joost, Eddie, 79
Jordan, Mike, 2
Jorgens, Arndt, 140
Joss, Addie, 35
Joyce, Bill, 8
Jude, Frank, 136
Junker, Lance, 16

Kaiser, Ken 101
Kaline, Al, 3
Kamenshek, Dottie, 84
Kaneda, Masaichi, 23, 28, 31
Karger, Ed, 36
Kazak, Eddie, 152
Keefe, Tim, 24, 26, 39
Keeler, Willie, 4, 18, 129
Kellum, Win, 101
Kelly, Honest John, 98
Kelly, King, 66
Kelly, Tom, 99
Kennedy, Bill, 29
Kennedy, Frosty, 10
Kent, Wes, 17
Killebrew, Harmon, 111
Killefer, Bill, 2
Kilroy, Matt, 25, 28
King, Richard, 133
Kingman, Dave, 13, 19, 88
Kinnaman, Bon, 150
Kipper, Bob, 33
Kirk, Jack, 154
Kittle, Hub, 138
Klein, Chuck, 16, 112
Klem, Bill, 97, 99, 102, 103
Knight, Ray, 11
Knott, Jack, 152
Koenig, Mark, 34
Konstanty, Jim, 111
Koufax, Sandy, 29, 34, 36,
    111, 113-114
Kuhualua, Fred, 134
Kunkel, Bill, 107
Kurowski, Whitey, 159

Lai, Buck, 134
Lajoie, Nap, 2, 3, 16, 50
Lake, Fred, 134
Lamb, Lyman, 6
Landes, Stan, 101
Lanier, Hal, 160
LaRoche, Dave, 39
Larsen, Don, 36, 114
Latham, Arlie, 145
Latina, Bud, 57
Lazzeri, Tony, 10, 59, 160
Lee, Scrip, 44, 106
Lefebvre, Bill, 12
LeJeune, Larry, 56
Lennon, Bill, 60
Lennon, Bob, 9
Leonard, Andy, 50

Leonard, Joe, 150
LeRoy, Louis, 136
Lewis, Allan, 61
Lezcano, Sixto, 76
Lincoln, Abraham, 131
Lindstrom, Axel, 140
Lipe, Perry, 110
Livingston, Jake, 139
Lobert, Hans, 63, 66
Lolich, Mickey, 114
Lombardi, Ernie, 111
Long, Dale, 11
Lopes, Davey, 61
Loucks, Scott, 88
Lowe, Bobby, 10
Lowrey, Peanuts, 152
Luciano, Ron, 101
Luderus, Fred, 78
Lum, Mike, 134
Lutz, Joe, 95
Luzinski, Greg, 19
Lyden, George, 150
Lynch, Tom, 107
Lynn, Fred, 110, 112, 114

Mabe, Bob, 158
Mack, Connie, 143, 144
MacMillan, Alexander, 38
MacPhail, Larry, 128
Madlock, Bill, 113
Magee, Sherry, 160
Magner, Stubby, 140
Malmquist, Walter, 1
Malone, Fergy, 55
Manning, Jack, 36
Mantle, Mickey, 16, 20, 76, 111
Marberry, Firpo, 36
Marichal, Juan, 113, 137
Marion, Marty, 111, 159
Maris, Roger, 9, 10, 76, 111
Marquard, Rube, 26
Marsans, Armando, 137
Martinez, Fred, 150
Masci, Enzo, 109
Mathews, Bobby, 31, 42
Mathewson, Christy, 24, 25, 41,
    151
Matlack, Jon, 113
Mauch, Gene, 143
May, Carlos, 125
Mays, Carl, 21, 43, 146
Mays, Willie, 3, 11, 111,
    112-113

Mazzilli, Lee, 62
McBride, Dick, 115
McBride, George, 78
McCarthy, Jack, 106
McCarthy, Joe, 143
McCarthy, John, 99
McCartney, Steve, 76
McCauley, Al, 47
McClain, Cliff, 64
McClellan, Bill, 55
McClellan, Dan, 36
McClelland, Tim, 101
McCormick, Barry, 107
McCormick, Frank, 111
McCovey, Willie, 111, 113
McCreary, Fred, 100
McDaniel, Lindy, 41
McDermott, Joe, 60
McDonald, Webster, 43-44
McDougald, Gil, 154
McEvoy, Lou, 34
McGill, Willie, 143
McGinley, Tim, 60
McGinnity, Joe, 43
McGlynn, Stoney, 25
McGowan, Bill, 97, 98, 103,
  160
McGraw, John, 143
McGrew, Slim, 141
McGuire, Deacon, 109
McKean, Jim, 101
McKechnie, Bill, 143
McKee, Red, 65
McKinley, Bill, 104
McLain, Denny, 111
McLean, Bill, 100
McManus, Marty, 84
McNair, Hurley, 106
McNulty, Bill, 76
McPhee, Bid, 57
McRae, Hal, 19
McSherry, John, 101
Meadows, Lee, 126
Medwick, Joe, 16, 111, 130
Mejias, Roman, 4
Mendez, Jose, 25, 87
Merullo, Lennie, 51
Meusel, Bob, 17
Meyers, Chief, 136
Michaels, Cass, 148
Michaelson, John, 140
Milan, Clyde, 78
Miller, Doggie, 50
Miller, Hack, 128

Miller, Henry, 14
Miller, Rick, 7
Milnar, Al, 42
Minetto, Craig, 92
Minoso, Minnie, 138
Mitchell, Jackie, 142
Mitchell, Willie, 31
Mizell, Wilmer, 139
Moeller, Danny, 78
Mohler, Kid, 55
Moore, Wilcy, 36
Moran, Charley, 107
Morgan, Eddie, 12
Morgan, Joe, 110, 113
Moriarty, George, 107
Morrissey, Chester, 156
Morrissey, Deacon, 140
Mota, Manny, 19-20
Mullane, Tony, 38, 56
Muller, Freddie, 79
Munn, Norman, 11
Munson, Thurman, 110, 150
Murakami, Masanori, 136-137
Murphy, Dale, 110
Murphy, Lizzie, 142
Murray, Miah, 107
Musial, Stan, 3, 111
Myers, Ken, 15
Myers, Ralph, 61

Nabors, Jack, 26
Nakano, Takeji, 97
Nash, Billy, 137
Nava, Sandy, 2
Naymick, Mike, 141
Neale, Greasy, 158
Necciai, Ron, 29
Ness, Jack, 4
Nettles, Graig, 88
Neudecker, Jerry, 105
Newcombe, Don, 21, 111
Newhouser, Hal, 111
Newman, Jack, 34
Newton, Doc, 25
Nichols. Kid, 24
Nicholson, Bill, 160
Nicholson, Dave, 13
Nicholson, Ovid, 61
Nickerson, Bobo, 54, 133
Nidegawa, Nobuaki, 97
Niekro, Phil, 41
Nieman, Bob, 12
Nixon, Donnell, 61

Nuxhall, Joe, 143

Oana, Henry, 134
O'Day, Hank, 19, 97, 107
Oeschger, Joe, 80
O'Farrell, Bob, 112
Oglesby, Jim, 4
Oh, Sadaharu, 8, 14, 17, 52
O'Hagan, Hal, 48
O'Leary, Dan, 64
Oliver, Al, 126
O'Neil, Buck, 144
O'Neill, Harry, 151
O'Neill, Tip, 134
O'Rourke, Frank, 2
O'Rourke, John, 7
Ortega, Phil, 136
Orth, Al, 107
Orwoll, Ossie, 87

Pahlman, Otto, 4
Paige, Satchel, 27, 138
Palmer, Dave, 36
Parker, Dave, 110, 113
Parnell, Mel, 42
Paskert, Dode, 38
Patkin, Max, 133
Patterson, Bob, 150
Pearce, Dickie, 80, 102
Pearce, Gracie, 2
Peck, Hal, 160
Peckinpaugh, Roger, 112, 145
Pellant, Gary, 20
Percival, Robert, 56
Perez, Tony, 1113
Perry, Gaylord, 24
Peters, Frank, 51
Pfeffer, Fred, 5-6
Pfeffer, Jeff, 148
Phillips, Bill, 134
Picetti, Vic, 150
Pierce, Bill, 106
Pieretti, Marino, 136
Pike, Lip, 137
Pinelli, Babe, 98, 107
Pipgras, George, 107
Plank, Eddie, 24
Podres, Johnny, 114
Porter, Darrell, 113
Postema, Pam, 102
Powell, Boog, 110
Powers, Mike, 150

Powers, Phil, 107
Price, Jackie, 133
Pryor, Paul, 98
Purnell, Benjamin, 87
Pytlak, Frankie, 53

Quigley, Ernie, 98, 101
Quinn, Jack, 13
Quinn, Joe, 89
Quisenberry, Dan, 37, 43

Radbourn, Old Hoss, 24, 29
Radcliff, John, 115
Raines, Larry, 95
Raines, Tim, 66
Ramsey, Toad, 28, 158-159
Raymond, Claude, 134
Reach, Al, 55, 115, 134
Reagan, Ronald, 132, 152
Redding, Cannonball Dick, 25
Redus, Gary, 1
Reese, Pee Wee, 22
Reid, Sandy, 101
Reilly, Long John, 17
Reiser, Pete, 122
Relford, Joe, 142
Remmerswaal, Wim, 92
Remsen, Jack, 127
Reynolds, Allie, 136
Reynolds, Tommie, 76
Rhines, Billy, 43
Rice, Grantland, 118
Rice, Jim, 19, 110
Richard, J.R., 34, 141
Richards, Paul, 38
Richardson, Bobby, 113-114
Richmond, Lee, 35
Rickey, Branch, 52, 122
Rigler, Cy, 97, 103
Rinaldi, Toro, 92
Ripken, Cal, 110
Risk, George, 150
Ritchey, Claude, 48
Rizzo, Angelo, 92
Rizzuto, Phil, 111
Roach, John, 38
Robertson, Charlie, 36
Robinson, Brooks, 45, 109, 111,
   113, 114
Robinson, Frank, 16, 111, 113,
   114, 144

Robinson, Jackie, 111, 131, 133, 160
Robinson, Wilbert, 5
Roebuck, Ed, 14
Roettger, Oscar, 32
Rogers, Tom, 147
Romano, Mike, 30
Rommel, Eddie, 41, 104, 107
Ronnenbergh, Martin, 92
Roosevelt, Franklin, 132
Rose, Don, 12
Rose, Eddie, 18
Rose, Pete, 3, 4, 6, 8, 20, 45, 109, 110, 114, 130
Rosen, Al, 111
Roseman, Chief, 137
Roush, Edd, 38
Roy, Charlie, 136
Rubio, Jorge, 38
Rudi, Joe, 45
Rue, Joe, 131
Ruffing, Red, 160
Runge, Paul, 101
Rusie, Amos, 31-32, 34
Russell, Gloria, 57
Ruth, Babe, 10, 14, 17, 55, 112, 130, 131, 142
Ryan, Johnny, 33
Ryan, Nolan, 28, 29, 31, 34, 35, 120
Ryan, Red, 41
Rye, Gene, 11, 15

Sain, Johnny, 21, 42
Sallee, Slim, 33
Sandburg, Ryne, 110
Sanner, Roy, 20
Santo, Ron, 160
Sauer, Hank, 111
Savage, Bob, 152
Sawyer, Carl, 132
Schacht, Al, 132
Schaefer, Germany, 64, 132
Schalk, Ray, 54
Schang, Wally, 127
Scheible, John, 28
Schlueter, Norm, 2
Schmelz, Gus, 127
Schmidt, Mike, 110, 114, 120
Schoendienst, Red, 154
Schriver, Pop, 54
Schulte, Bob, 32
Schulte, Frank, 112

Schwert, Pius, 139
Score, Herb, 154
Seaver, Tom, 30, 88
Secory, Frank, 98, 107
Selkirk, George, 134
Sensenderfer, Count, 115
Sewell, Joe, 18
Sewell, Rip, 39
Shantz, Bobby, 111
Shaw, Dupee, 28
Shepard, Bert, 156
Sheridan, Jack, 105
Sherry, Larry, 114, 115
Shindle, Bill, 49
Shocker, Urban, 39
Shore, Ernie, 35
Shotten, Burt, 144
Sicking, Eddie, 78
Siewert, Ralph, 141
Sigman, Sanford, 51
Sipek, Dick, 157
Sisler, George, 2, 3, 112
Skowron, Bill, 76
Slaybaugh, Bob, 158
Smith, Vinnie, 107
Smithson, Mike, 141
Snyder, Pop, 54, 107
Sockalexis, Louis, 66, 135-136
Soden, Arthur, 118
Somers, Al, 103
Soto, Mario, 31
Spahn, Warren, 24, 41
Spalding, Al, 25, 26, 57, 83, 89, 92
Sparks, Baxter, 25
Speaker, Tris, 3, 6, 112
Sprinz, Joe, 53
Squires, Mike, 56
Staggs, Steve, 88
Stanley, Mickey, 45
Stanton, Lefty, 33
Starfin, Victor, 24-25, 139
Stargell, Willie, 110, 114
Start, Joe, 109
Staub, Rusty, 19
Stearns, Dan, 137
Stengel, Casey, 143
Stennett, Rennie, 5
Stephens, Gene, 5-6
Stern, Bill, 118
Stivetts, Jacks, 21
Stone, Jeff, 61
Stone, Toni, 142
Stotz, Carl, 120

Stovey, Harry, 10
Strand, Paul, 3
Stratton, Monty, 156
Street, Gabby, 54
Stricklett, Elmer, 43
Strief, George, 8
Stuart, Dick, 9, 13
St. Vrain, Jim, 64
Suder, Pete, 79
Sudol, Ed. 98
Sugiura, Tadashi, 25
Sullivan Billy, 54
Sullivan, Joe, 49
Sullivan, Tom, 88
Summers, Bill, 98, 99
Summers, Ed, 41
Sunday, Billy, 63
Sunkel, Tom, 158
Sutter, Bruce, 37
Suttles, Mule, 10
Sutton, Don, 113
Swanson, Evar, 63, 66
Swartwood, Ed, 107
Sweeney, Bill, 29
Sweeney, Charlie, 29
Sylvester, Lou, 140

Taft, William, 132
Takahashi, Hiroshi, 136
Tanaka, Tatsuhiko, 136
Tannehill, Lee, 48
Tanner, Chuck, 12
Tate, Pop, 55
Taylor, Harry, 79
Taylor, Luther, 157
Tayson, Johnny, 95
Tebbetts, Birdie, 57
Tenace, Gene, 47, 114
Tener, John, 139
Terry, Bill, 2
Terry, Ralph, 114
Thayer, Fred, 58
Thomas, Bill, 23, 26
Thomas, Gorman, 39, 76
Thomas, Reggie, 51
Thompson, Jeff, 34
Thompson, Sam, 75
Thorpe, Jim, 66, 135-136
Tincup, Ben, 135-136
Titus, John, 127
Toporcer, Specs, 126
Torre, Joe, 110

Tovar, Cesar, 51
Trammell, Alan, 113
Travis, Cecil, 151
Trout, Dizzy, 18
Troy, Bun, 41, 150-151
Trucks, Virgil, 29
Truman, Harry, 132
Tucker, Tommy, 20
Turley, Bob, 114
Tyng, Jim, 58

Uhle, George, 21, 42
Unglaub, Bob, 53
Urbanus, Han, 29, 92
Uremovich, Mike, 51

Vance, Dazzy, 87, 112
Vander Meer, Johnny, 35
Van Haltren, George, 32
Venzon, Tony, 104
Vernon, Mickey, 47
Versalles, Zoilo, 111
Viau, Lee, 140
Vickers, Rube, 25, 29, 36
Vico, George, 12
Voiselle, Bill, 126
Vollmer, Clyde, 12

Wagner, Honus, 3, 62, 64, 129, 130
Wagner, Leon, 113
Waitkus, Eddie, 153
Waits, Bobby, 51
Waitt, Charlie, 57
Walker, Dixie, 87
Walker, Fleet, 133
Walker, Welday, 133
Walsh, Ed, 14, 25
Walters, Bucky, 7, 111
Waner, Paul, 3, 112
Wantz, Dick, 150
Ward, John M., 25, 35
Warneke, Lon, 99, 107
Warner, John, 49
Washington, Herb, 66
Washington, Jap, 106
Waterman, Fred, 115
Watkins, Bill, 134
Watson, Bob, 60
Webb, Earl, 7

INDEX

Weintraub, Phil, 54
Welch, Mickey, 19, 24, 30, 41
Wells, Willie, 22
Wendelstedt, Harry, 103
Werber, Fred, 62
Werden, Perry, 10
Wever, Stefan, 141
Weyand, Ron, 51
Weyer, Lee, 101
Whistler, Lew, 50
White, Will, 126
Wiggs, Jimmy, 140
Wilhelm, Hoyt, 23, 41
Wilhelm, Irvin, 27
Wilhoit, Joe, 4
Williams, Bill, 104
Williams, Charlie, 100
Williams, Cy, 52
Williams, Nature Boy, 133
Williams, R.P., 64
Williams, Smokey Joe, 30, 34, 40
Williams, Ted, 2, 16, 52, 111
Williamson, Ned, 5-6, 10
Wills, Maury, 63, 111, 113
Wilson, Eddie, 148
Wilson, Fred, 133
Wilson, Hack, 15
Wilson, Jim, 153

Wilson, Jud, 1
Wilson, Owen, 8
Wilson, Willie, 20, 66
Wilson, Woodrow, 132
Winfield, Dave, 88
Witt, Mike, 36
Wren, Christine, 102
Wright, George, 59, 82, 115
Wright, Harry, 39, 82
Wynn, Early, 24
Wysong, Biff, 87

Yastrzemski, Carl, 3, 16, 109, 111, 113
Yeager, Joe, 147
Yeager, Steve, 114
Yellowhorse, Chief, 136
Yokely, Laymon, 25
Yonamine, Wally, 135
Young, Cy, 23, 26, 35
Yount, Robin, 110

Zabel, Zip, 37
Zarefoos, Mike, 53
Zimmer, Don, 154
Zimmerman, Heinie, 16